MONEY TRADE STOCKS

JACOB DAVID

DISCLAIMER:
This book was researched and written by Jacob David. The author is not responsible for any wrong investment decisions anyone makes. Do your own research on every stock, each time, before you invest your money.
No part of this book may be copied, reproduced or reprinted without the permission of the author.
All materials in this book are copyrighted.
Author, Jacob David. Second edition © 2020.

MONEY TRADE STOCKS
JACOB DAVID

LEGAL DISCLAIMER

LIMIT OF LIABILITY/DISCLAIMER OF WARRANTY: While Jacob David, the author of "Money Trade Stocks" has made his best efforts in preparing this book, he makes no express representations or warranties with respect to the 100% accuracy or completeness of the content and market information presented herein. The advice and strategies for stock market trading in this book are to be used at each trader's discretion. The author, Jacob David shall not be liable in any form or manner, for all losses or profits incurred or any other financial form of damage, inclusive, but not limited to special, incidental, or consequential incurred due to trading.

Trading in the stock market is not a get rich quick scheme. It requires education, dedication and daily perseverance, along with careful investing of your money based on consulting trading select charts which involves high or low probabilities and percentages for success. The stock market can change at anytime, day, without warning. These percentages and probabilities are calculated by your broker's systems based on normal market conditions. Any change in those variables in market conditions can bring profit or loss to your account portfolio. The purpose of this book is to educate and inform all readers who buy this book, and make them more confident in buying and selling stocks at their discretion, only after proper research. Each trader assumes full responsibility for his or her own trading.

ISBN # 9781075492464

MONEY TRADE STOCKS
JACOB DAVID

Date Published: July 2019

AUTHOR'S NOTE

Thank you for buying this book.

This book seeks to educate beginners and intermediate stock investors. It provides a good introduction to the stock market, especially for those who want to begin investing, those who have been waiting on the sidelines, without access to help and information, and for interested students.

I realize your time is valuable. You want to get down to learning all about trading stocks, right away. That's what I intend to do - to get to the heart of the matter.

Please remember to rate my book honestly on what you feel, how much this book has helped you expand your understanding of the stock market. I so much appreciate your feedback on this book. Please email me at: Creative ads for you @ yahoo.com

I have answered a few personal questions towards the end of this book.

Thank you once again,

MONEY TRADE STOCKS
JACOB DAVID

Jacob David.

Introduction:

➤ Who is this book for?

This book is for the beginner and intermediate level stock market learners, and those who want to fill in gaps in their understanding about the stock market.

➤ I've heard people say investing in stocks is a blind gamble. Is this true?

To gamble is to take a chance on something that has the possibility of going either way, with a 50-50 chance of winning or losing. The outcome is never certain. Examples of such gambling are: Card games, Casino games, Lottery, Horse racing, and betting on Sports.

With horse racing and sports, there's a track record of the horses or athletes you can rely on, which makes it more scientific, as you use historical data to place a calculated bet, which increases your chances of winning or doubling your bet. Those who care not to do their research have a greater chance of losing.

When you invest in the stock market it's doing so after doing your research on the stocks you intend to buy. As you will see later on in this book, there are several items on a checklist a trader has to consider before he or she decides to invest their money and purchase shares of any stock.

Based on historical data patterns and indicator charts, they let you know if the price chart of a stock is in an uptrend or downtrend, along with several other factors, the trader (you) take an educated, calculated risk on the stock. This is why investing in the stock market is not a blind gamble.

➤ What is trading stocks?

Trading stocks are the buying and selling of company shares for determined profit. Your set profit percentage can range between 3% to 10%. You do not have to hold a stock for eternity. If you'd like, you can exit in a month, or six months, or 12 months, when your goal of 10% is realized, provided you watch your stock rise carefully to your desired profit level.

If you find that the stock is not strong enough to rise up to 10% of profit level, sell at 7% profit level, and find another stock to trade. What matters is that you do not fall in love with any one stock. Keep stock trading unemotional at best, as far as possible.

Always remember, you are here to invest your money for a definite profit, to grow your money, also known as R.O.I (return on your investment). Also, do not get emotionally invested into your stock. Like someone said, "Do not get married to a stock."

➤ Why must I invest in good company stocks?

You can invest in good company stocks for any number of reasons. But the primary reason should be to make money. The reasons to make money should be to support your family, fund your children's education, support your retirement years, and all the while donating 10% of your earnings to help the suffering and underprivileged people in the world.

MONEY TRADE STOCKS
JACOB DAVID

If you invested your money, say $1000, untouched, in a savings account in a bank for one full year, at the end of the year, you may get $1020/- at 2% return if you put it in a special investment vehicle, say a certificate of deposit (CD).

If the same money was invested into a well researched stock of a company, the money of $1,000 could turn into $1,500 or more in just 6 months. That is a 50% return in 6 months averaging 8.33% return each month. Now this return is possible, if this stock is a solid stock with a great reputation and has good earnings.

See the difference of how investing into a stock market, with careful preparation can reward your efforts? It's better than investing in a bank where your money does not work for you.

Real Example: Amazon (AMZN) went public in 1997 at $18 per share. So, let's say you invested $1000 and purchased Amazon back in 1997. At $18 a share, you would have bought 55 shares (not including any commissions).

If you were a conservative investor and held on to those shares, because you believed in the CEO, Jeff Bezos and his company, his visions and goals, and you held it long enough to 2019, today's value is $1823.28 per share. That is $1805.28 increase per share, increasing $82.05 per year, per share, for 22 years.

So your 55 Amazon shares would be valued at $100,280.40 giving you a **10,000% increase** for your $1000 investment in 22 years. That is a **454% increase each year** on your $1000 initial investment.

Meanwhile, the bank in 22 years would have with 2% interest compounded annually, returned your $1000 (no additional money made) to roughly $1,545.98, a negative difference of $98,734.42 when comparing it with Amazon's 55 shares. (Compound interest calculator keyword search - moneychimp.com) Recent stock analysis of Amazon holds the view that a single share of AMZN can reach $3,000 by the end of 2021.

This above example is in the single case of Amazon. There have been cases of many companies failing badly and going out of business in just five to ten years because of mismanagement.

It is therefore advisable to watch your stock and pay attention to the health of the company constantly as the value of your stock grows.

Hope this answer has convinced you why you must seriously consider investing in good company stocks.

Remember, it's never too late to start.

➤ What online communities can help me learn and solidify my trading strategies?

*Important websites to visit and learn.

Google these sites below and bookmark them. Use them as needed to become an expert in stocks and options. Make it a point to visit these websites once in 3 days.

- Benzinga - Market news, analysis.
- Bio-pharm Catalyst
- ETF (.com)

- Finviz S&P 500 Map (has Heat map)*
- Investopedia - learn all you can.
- Macro Trends
- Market Beat
- Market Watch
- Morningstar - Independent research.
- Nasdaq
- Seeking Alpha - stocks on the move.
- Select Sector Spider's.*
- Simply Wall St.
- Stocktwits (Tweets about stocks).
- Yahoo Finance
- Zacks stock research

Some of these sites above may ask you to take a membership. They provide limited features with a free profile. You may do so at your discretion. Always seek to add to this list as you learn about stocks and go forward in life.

Some of these sites may promote certain stocks, you have to do your own research to sort out what is real and what is "hype."

Example: A website can say that stock XYZ has 5 positive Analyst BUY recommendations. Check with your broker platform, and other websites, to see if this is really true .

MONEY TRADE STOCKS
JACOB DAVID

On **Stocktwits** my username is **JacobD70**.

* Heat Map (see page 11).

➤ What TV channels analyze the stock market?

Bloomberg TV - deals with the stock market and world markets, including the European markets.

CNBC. The U.S stock market analysis is on through the day, on weekdays.

➤ What is a stock market **heat map**?

On the Select Sector Spiders* (Spdrs) website, you will see Select Sector SPDR Tools. Under it, click on View Full Sector Tracker. Then click on Sector Heat Map. The Heat Map shows Green, Red and Gray colors of the 11 major sectors in the stock market. Gray color is no change. Green is bullish trend. Red is bearish trend. On the top you can select the time frame from 1 Day to 5 years. This will help you gauge the market psychology over the period of time selected.

➤ Why is the **Sector heat map** so important?

It is advisable to look at the heat map each day, preferably in the evening, in preparation for the next day's trading. The heat map gives you a bird's eye view of how the stock market is performing. You can narrow down on the sector(s) that is performing well to further narrow down on individual stocks in that sector. Viewing the heat map makes your job for searching stocks easier.

➤ What are the major U.S Stock market crashes? (Knowing history helps).

One of the biggest risks of trading in the stock market is the possibility of a market crash. Painful lessons from history have created checks and balances in the stock market that can reduce the impact on shareholders from such a crash. It's good to learn a bit of the history of the stock market failures, so read on.

MONEY TRADE STOCKS
JACOB DAVID

The first stock market crash of October 1929 happened because the stock market was doing so well. A "roaring" market is what they called it. People were so heady and confident, that they borrowed a lot of money to trade in the stock market, speculating that the stocks will climb higher. When this illusion suddenly popped, the value of the stocks went South, it was the biggest crash that happened. People were left clueless as to what happened, they were left holding worthless stock paper, also called as "bag holders." The Investors could not pay back their debts and several of them went into bankruptcy. Greed was what took over and ruined everything.

The second stock market crash also took place in October 1987, called "Black Monday." There were rampant speculations and heavy buying, traders leveraged borrowed money and added to this mix was technology. People traded and betted on junk bonds and used margin accounts to finance their trades. Improved computer systems made it easy to trade fast and furious, and many of them did not see the cliff coming, they drove right over it, plunging into the abyss (metaphorically). The stock market plunged 23% and many stocks lost their value.

The third stock market crash took place between 1999 and 2000, because of the Dot Com bubble. Investors took to favoring the Technology sector over the others. Many IPO's (Initial Public Offerings) took place in this sector and investors clamored to buy these stocks, without doing proper research into the companies. Many companies soon lost their value because they did not have a strong operational foundation, crashed and burned. Many investors lost their money.

This crash happened because investors favored one sector over all others, second, they did not do proper research on the companies, and third, they wanted quick, overnight returns.

The fourth and final major stock market crash took place in 2008 and carried on well into 2009. The 2008 collapse happened due to rampant greed and extreme dishonesty, to put it mildly.

Mortgage backed stocks which were backed by the U.S housing sector, were sold by financial institutions to investors. These mortgages were sold to American families in large numbers, whose financial and job backgrounds these financial institutions never verified. The banks and certified lender institutions gave these families loans to make the sale of homes possible, knowing fully well, that one day, these families will in the near future foreclose on their homes. When this happened, it was the largest "housing bubble" that popped. The impact of this nearly devastated the country.

The crash was so bad that the government had to step in to federally fund huge banks that were left with worthless, unpaid mortgages. Interest rates were lowered to zero. Many homes were foreclosed upon. Many American families could not pay their mortgages. They had to short sale their home, agreeing to sell the home for far less than what the home was worth, just to fulfill their debt obligations to the bank. It was a field day for private investors who grabbed homes for pennies on the dollar, invested in these homes, fixed them up and flipped them for huge profits.

Each of these four stock market crashes have taught the country and stock traders valuable lessons. The monetary losses slowed down the market by an average of five to ten years each time a crash happened. The stock market took those five to ten years to recover from these huge financial losses.

➤ What is historically the worst month for stock trading?

Historically, September is considered a bad month for trading stocks. This is general consensus held by the public.

➤ What is the minimum money that I need to invest in stocks?

People can start off with as low as $250 to $500/- But long before you do this, carefully study the market, make notes, study which sectors you like, and why, which stocks you'd like to buy shares in. Certain brokers have deposit minimums. Do your research on brokers, their requirements, and ask other traders on social media or forums about their trading experiences on different broker platforms. Don't fall in love with a certain sector just because your mom, dad, uncle, boyfriend, or best friend works in that sector. That's just being plain amateurish.

➤ When can I start investing in stocks?

You can start investing as soon as you become confident in yourself. By "confident" I mean, you know what you are doing, have the learning to back you up. So learn by watching the stock market, engage in discussions, read up on the stock market, learn to gauge market sentiment regularly, study catalysts, analyze the stock technicals, all of which are necessary to execute a successful trade. Always have a plan, know where to enter, and when to exit.

Long term investing is different. You can hold a stock as long as the company is healthy in its finances, product/service offerings, and daily operations.

➤ Is it good to discuss stocks with family and friends?

It's best not to discuss your trades with friends in your social circles and family members, but observe social sentiment on websites. Try your best to discuss the stock market in general terms or listen when they discuss specific companies, when the subject comes up at family parties.

Discussing your trades with friends who don't trade or do not keep in touch with the stock market, can give rise to misleading multiple opinions, which can cause you to be double minded, inactive, and useless, waiting on the sidelines.

There is an exception to the above rule. If a family member or friend(s) can be mature about the stock market, is knowledgeable about the stock market, an active participant in the market, is presently trading, and has made good returns, good experience, you could discuss your trades with him or her. Consider him or her to be your trade mentor after much careful thought.

➤ Should I listen to my gut feeling?

After doing your research, if you feel confident, go ahead and buy your shares, with a plan on when to exit or hold long term for a few years.

MONEY TRADE STOCKS
JACOB DAVID

If there is a nagging feeling in the pit of your stomach, or some unexplainable feeling that makes you overly cautious, listen to that inner voice. Find another stock to invest. It's always better to do this than lose money.

Here's my **real life anecdote** on why you should listen to your gut feeling: The price of **Ford (F)** had fallen from $12.97, February 9, 2005 to $1.88 on February 9, 2009, when the stock market tanked, due to the nationwide Housing Mortgage crisis. I decided to purchase 1000 shares at $1.88 for a total of $1880.

I studied the stock market and economy at large. The U.S. government had offered an $80.7 billion bailout to the auto industry, in layers, which lasted from Dec. 2008 to Dec. 2014. Ford did not accept the bailout, while others did. Ford however accepted $9 Billion from the government and invested another $5 Billion for a total of $14B in new technologies.

However, I made the mistake of discussing my trade with some stock analyst expert, a lady, who happened to call me one fine day. I told her I was planning on investing $2K in Ford.

She went off for a good ten minutes on how wrong it would be to invest my money and possibly lose it all, since the auto industry was in a recession, and on and on, she went. So she ended up convincing me. And so, I did not buy Ford (F).

On March 9, 2010, exactly a year and one month later, the prices of Ford (F) shares were trading at $12.66. If I would have purchased 1000 shares of Ford (F), my profit would have been $10,780 ($12,660 - $1880). I still happen to remember this clearly, how some so called stock expert talked me out of investing, even after I had done my research. So, YES, listen to your gut.

And whatever happens after that, good or bad, is solely upon you. At least you'd have the satisfaction of having listened to your gut.

➤ How do I really learn the stock market?

This is called "immersive learning." You have to remember that trading in stocks takes a lifetime. So remember to do these actions consistently, in manageable pieces, making sure not to burn yourself out in the process.

Consider this, "*Stock trading is a slow, daily marathon, not a sprint.*" You have a long way to go, so pace yourself in your daily learning. Don't overdo your learning, as you may soon give up and hate stocks forever.

Here's what you can do daily, in small bite size pieces:

1. Read daily news on the market.
2. Read short reputable trade blogs.
3. Research on individual companies.
4. Read select books on trading.
5. Watch short videos on trading.
6. Keep notes on what you learn.
7. Look at stock SEC filings, insider trades.
8. Study Financial Reports for stocks.
9. Learn how to analyze a stock.
10. Focus on well-performing sectors and stocks by each quarter.
11. Try to attend earnings calls and announcements for healthy stocks.
12. Study the competition for each stock.

MONEY TRADE STOCKS
JACOB DAVID

Slowly build your tolerance for the stock market, and your brain's capacity to accept live charts, figures, percentages, ratios, historical charts, stock screeners, and much more.

➤ How can I build a tolerance for stock trading? What are some of the exercises you recommend doing?

Learn to have an affinity toward numbers. When bored, having nothing to do, switch off your TV and do the following:

Find online games that involve math and numbers.

Do some random percentage calculations.

Go online and read stock news.

Check on different stock sectors daily.

Read up on what analysts are saying about different stocks on reputable websites.

Play with the stock screeners and try various combinations of setting them up.

Click on Historical quotes and learn the price performance of stock prices for select stocks.

Visit Stock market forums to glance, read stock market sentiment. Remember some can be skewed or manipulative.

View different stock charts and play with your platform settings. See how stocks perform daily.

Doing these activities randomly but repeatedly will gradually help your mind focus on the stock markets and related activities.

➤ What if I don't have time to stock trade?

This is a common problem many new and existing traders face. It's quite normal and sometimes overwhelming when traders get started, trying to trade stocks. To overcome this, I recommend doing the following steps:

1. Check how many activities you do each day and on weekends. Write them down.

2. Find out which of these activities are not productive. Some are totally wasteful.

3. Try to trim or cut out these activities in their entirety.

4. Exchange this time to learn about stocks and the nuances of trading.

5. When you can, paper trade, to get used to the broker's platform. Take a few months to get the hang of things.

6. When you are ready and confident, find out if you can set the trade in the evenings. Ask your broker on how to set the trade.

7. Set short bursts of time, 5 to 10 minutes each day to research stocks. Make note of ticker symbols of stocks that look promising to provide good returns.

8. Invest only in solid blue chip stocks, as you may not have time during the day to keep watch over the stocks. Stable stocks cause less worries and also helps keep your money safe in the long run.

9. Check news on your individual stocks and see if you can take 5 minutes during your lunch hour to place a "sell" or "buy" trade using the trade app supplied by your broker.

10. Find ways to read at least one page of a stock book per day. Then think about what you have read.

11. Find time, try to reduce other secondary activities in order to exchange those times to learn and do trading.

12. Keep a notebook with brief daily notes for future reference.

Getting started:

➤ What are "stocks"?

Stocks are collections of shares that belong to various companies. When you purchase a stock (as less as 1 share or 10,000 shares) you get part ownership of that company.

MONEY TRADE STOCKS
JACOB DAVID

As a stockholder, you get to participate in the company's good and bad aspects of growth, its profits and losses, you get to cast votes on decisions regards its broad operations.

In exchange for your money, you get a percentage equity in the company. You get to buy limited shares in exchange for your money, based on the stock price.

➤ What are "shares"?

A share is one unit of the company that gives you one unit ownership in that company. Each share is traded/exchanged for a set dollar value.

The company is looking to raise capital for its operations from the public through the selling of its shares. So the officers/board of directors decide on how much the company needs to raise. Then they divide this total capital into equal parts, which is known as one share.

A share may start at $1 or $303,000 per unit of share, as in the case of Berkshire Hathaway Class A Stock. Ticker symbol (BRK.A).

➤ What is a "Ticker Symbol" ?

A ticker symbol is a set of letters that represent the stock of the company. In the case of Walmart Stores, the ticker symbol is WMT. When you use this ticker symbol in recording your thoughts in social media comments, do so by doing this - **$WMT** which helps bold the ticker symbol. (Stock Twits - social media).

➤ What is a "float"?

The "Float" is the total number of shares made available by the company to the public for trading.

➤ What is a "Low Float" stock?

A low float stock is when a company releases a relatively low number of shares to the public for trading. Because of a limited supply of shares, the demand for this stock can shoot up, if there is positive news or event happening at the company.

MONEY TRADE STOCKS
JACOB DAVID

➤ What is a stock split?

A stock split can leave the shareholder with more units of shares. A 2-for-1 or 3-for-1 split would mean the shareholder will now have 2 or 3 additional shares for every unit share she previously owned. Stock splits are seen as positive, as the shareholder now owns more equity or percentage in the company. Also, this brings in more buyers. A stock split could make the company more valuable, if it has a good track record for growth and expansion.

➤ What is a "reverse-split" ?

A reverse-split means shares are merged to form fewer shares. Sometimes, shares are merged with the unit share gaining a higher value. But what really happens is the shareholder is left holding fewer units of shares after a reverse split occurs. A 1-for-2 reverse split would mean you end up owning 50 shares when you actually had 100 shares, with a slightly higher price on the 50 shares. In essence, you will lose some money in the process.

➤ What is the Bid/Ask price for a stock?

If you are buying a stock you will have to pay the **Ask price**. The Ask price is what sellers are willing to accept for each share unit.

If there is not much demand for the stock, you may try the **price slider** to offer the Mid Price or the Natural price (normal ask) or set the slider to any price in between. This then becomes a Limit order, and in some cases, it gets accepted, if demand is low. This means you have essentially save some money at entry, plus really save on trade commissions by offering a lower price per share unit.

The **Bid price** for a stock is what you will receive when you sell the shares of the stock and exit. The Bid price is always lower than the Ask price.

➤ What is Bid/Ask size?

The Bid/Ask size helps you measure demand and supply for a stock. If demand and supply are neck and neck, this will increase volatility for the stock as well.

MONEY TRADE STOCKS
JACOB DAVID

Each stock has the Bid/Ask size. If the Bid/Ask size are equal, there is normalcy in trade. If the Bid size is higher than the Ask size, this means there is more demand for the shares, created by the buyers and vice versa.

Bid = Demand
Ask = Supply

This is essentially Demand vs Supply. This changes daily.

Let's look at some **real life examples**:

GE - General Electric, B/A Size: 400x36,000.

F - Ford, B/A Size: 17,300x1,500.

NVDA - Nvidia Corp, B/A Size: 800x100.

AAPL - Apple Inc, B/A Size: 300x200.

BYND - Beyond Meat B/A Size: 200x200.

(Bid/Ask size recorded as of June 2019).

MONEY TRADE STOCKS
JACOB DAVID

➤ What is a "Catalyst"? How are share prices impacted by this?

A Catalyst is "the messenger that brings certain changes." In the case of stocks for companies, daily positive news or event happenings at these companies can boost the price of the shares. If the news is negative, the price of shares can plummet or drop like a rock. Another expression is "the falling knife."

➤ What are some examples of a catalyst?

1. Earnings announcement.
2. Company releases new invention.
3. Company gets new medicine approved by the FDA.
4. Company sending medicine to clinical trials.
5. Company expanding business abroad.
6. Company hires proven expert as a consultant to distribute products.
7. Company's medicine shows positive test results (Phase 3).
8. Company raises more capital.
9. Company is getting acquired by another bigger company.

10.   Company is acquiring another proven company with strong revenue.
11.   Company adds on service or product lines that will increase sales and ultimately revenue for shareholders.

➤ Who else may purchase stock of a company other than the public?

The company's Board of Directors, employees, or group purchase can be done known under the Employee stock ownership plan, banks, large trading brokers, hedge fund managers, can purchase stocks of a company.

➤ What are the different economic sectors of the stock market?

Sectors are broadly classified according to the Global Industry Classification Standard (GICS). This helps make it uniform and trading easier across the world.

The GICS was developed together by the Morgan Stanley Capital International (MSCI) and Standard & Poor 500 (S&P 500)

There are **11 broad economic sectors**, which are:

- Consumer Discretionary
- Consumer Staples
- Energy
- Financials
- Health Care
- Industrials
- Information Technology
- Materials
- Real Estate
- Telecommunication Services
- Utilities

Under these 11, are 24 industry groups, 68 industries, and 157 sub-industries.

To study these in detail, go on a stock screener with your broker and spend 15 minutes a day, studying stocks in sectors that really interest you. Don't overdo this, as it could burn you out mentally.

Make brief typed or handwritten notes as you go, and this will help you deepen your understanding of the sectors, sub-sectors, and specific stocks in specific industries.

Be sure to date your notes each day, and you will notice progress in your daily analysis. This is important to do, as it will encourage you mentally, as you learn about the stock market.

No matter how experienced you become, still keep the habit of writing brief notes daily. Never give up this habit.

➤ What is a "day trade"?

A day trade is when a trader buys and sells shares in the same day. Usually the trader trades 4 to 5 times during the week. Different brokers have restrictions on Capital requirements for day trading. In most cases, a minimum of $25K is required to be exempt from any restrictions on the number of day trades you can do per week.

➤ What are the limitations day traders put on themselves?

Day traders usually find they have limited capital. Most times, their capital can get tied up in different stocks if they are not in the habit of regularly taking profits, choosing bad stocks, and rearranging their portfolio.

Day traders stop advancing themselves by not learning further about stocks on weekends or in their downtime. Education has to be on a daily basis. The trader has to pace himself or herself.

Day traders do limited research on the stocks they plan to trade. They sometimes skip screening stocks stop looking at the technicals, industry competition, and don't read the SEC filings for the stocks.

Day traders are humans too. They often times get burned out if they focus on way too many stocks, without a clear focus or plan on how to trade them.

➤ What is "after-hours" trading? (EXT)

The stock market trades 5 minutes after it closes each business day. Trades that happen after 4:05 PM E.S.T, are registered as "after-hours" or "extended hours" trading. Stock prices tend to go up after hours, if EARNINGS beat analyst estimates, or gets positive news. Sometimes share prices fall steeply after the market closes, if the company gets bad news or poor earnings. If it is bad news, stock prices always tend to adjust themselves in the following days, unless the news is SO bad, that the stock is unlikely to recover. That rarely happens.

➤ How do stock prices go up or down? Who controls the price of a stock?

The public market controls the price of each stock trading on the exchange. Demand and Supply is created in the market, based on various factors - company performance, positive or negative news, assets, liabilities, earnings each quarter, and a host of other aspects that determine if the price of a stock goes up or down. If buyers are willing to pay increasing increments of money to buy shares, the prices go up. If they retain their shares, and do not sell, then prices shoot up.

If sellers start selling or dumping shares, due to unexpected low earnings or bad news, this can tank or crash the stock price in a flash. This happens during stock earnings season.

➤ What is a "swing trade" ?

A swing trade could mean the trader buys a stock and holds it for a few days before he sells it. Sometimes, traders wait for up to 2 weeks to get a better return as the price of the stock climbs up. It is advisable for traders to check the health of their stocks daily.

➤ What is "market cap" ?

Market cap is short for "Market Capitalization." This is the amount that the company is actually seeking to raise by selling the public its shares. Market capitalization is arrived at multiplying one unit of share by the total number of outstanding shares in the market.

For example: (As of May 25, 2019)

BE (Bloom Energy) has 60 Million shares outstanding. Present value of one share is $11.17. Market cap is therefore, 670.4 Million. (Manufactures solid fuel cells).

BAC (Bank of America) has 9.5 Billion shares outstanding. Present value of one share is $28.18. Market cap is therefore, $267.9 Billion.

See the difference between both stocks, how Bank of America's market cap is in the Billions, compared to Bloom Energy, which is in the Millions.

➤ What is "Market Value" of a company?

Market value is different from Market Cap of a stock. Market value of a company is calculated by looking into a company's financials, its daily operations, present and future demand of its products and services.

A lot of variables go into calculating the Market value of a company. What's most important is the "Operating Capital" available for the company to run its operations for that year. Next is "Assets" that a company owns or has recently acquired. Next is "Intellectual Property" that a company owns or has recently acquired.

MONEY TRADE STOCKS
JACOB DAVID

A company's debts are seen as negative. It can seriously hamper daily operations and hurt the value of the stock badly.

➤ What are a company's "assets" ?

Anything that the company owns and is tangible with positive benefits are known as assets.

The assets of a company increase value and stability of the stock. Assets can be:

- Cash and cash equivalents.
- Outstanding stocks.
- Prepaid Insurance.
- Existing inventory.
- Patents, Intellectual property.
- Office Buildings.
- Plant and plant Equipment.
- Transportation.
- Accounts receivable.
- Investments made for expansion.

Some assets like transportation (includes private Jets, Trucks) depreciating assets.

MONEY TRADE STOCKS
JACOB DAVID

Real estate property can have both depreciating and appreciating qualities.

➤ What are a company's "Liabilities" ?

Liabilities are considered "risks" to the company's investments that impacts the stock's value.

- Debts the company has taken.
- Mortgages on real estate holdings.
- Deferred or Lost revenues.
- Accrued Operating expenses.
- Outstanding equipment leases.
- Damages incurred. (all types).

➤ What is the "annual financial report" ?

The annual financial report includes the company's performance, financial health, board decisions on growth/expansion plans for the next year. This report is shared publicly with the shareholders first and to the general public who wants to study their chances of investing in the company.

MONEY TRADE STOCKS
JACOB DAVID

The financial summary includes positive cash flow, active loans/debts, trends in sales earnings via products and services, recording of assets and liabilities.

➤ What is a "quarter" ?

A quarter is 3 months. There are four quarters to the year, totaling 12 months. Standard quarters for companies is when they report earnings in March, June, September and December.

➤ What is known as "market sentiment" ?

The shares of different companies in the stock market is being traded by live human beings. Market sentiment is the collective attitude of all these traders, reacting to market news of the day, company performance, global trade tensions, political news, which result in buying and selling stocks of various companies, that belong to different economic sectors.

➤ What are some of the top stock brokers who can help you trade stocks?

MONEY TRADE STOCKS
JACOB DAVID

Some of the best stock brokers are: (arranged alphabetically)

- Charles Schwab
- E-Trade
- Fidelity Investments
- Interactive Brokers
- Merrill Edge
- TradeStation
- TD Ameritrade

The above list is based on a general consensus of the top stock brokers in the market. Charles Schwab acquired TD Ameritrade on November 25, 2019 for $26 Billion all-stock deal.

➤ What happened to commissions for trading stocks?

Brokers made money each time you bought and sold a stock (a collection of shares) knowns as a trading commission. Some brokers charge you $0.005, half a penny per share, per trade, while some charge you $6.95 to $9.95. Some brokers charge you $10 as inactivity fee each month, if you don't trade for 30 days or more. As of **December 2019**, all trade fees for major brokers were eliminated due to fierce competition to gain public trust and business.

➤ Once I sell a stock, how long will it take for the funds to find its way back to my account?"

Some brokers take up to 3 days to settle the funds into your account. If this trade amount was $10,000, then you'd be waiting for 3 days before you carry out your next trade, which is a big time waster, if you were planning to buy another great stock right away, as soon as you exited the other stock.

Brokers like TD Ameritrade and Charles Schwab should have funds ready at once for trading.

➤ What are "bull" and "bear" markets? How did they come to be named that way?

Bull and bear markets represent the behavior and characteristics of these two animals.

A bull is aggressive by nature. A bull charges. A bull thrusts its horns upward while in attack mode. So also, a bull market charges up on an upward trend.

A bear hibernates or goes to sleep for up to 7.5 months. A bear moves slowly. A bear swipes it's paw downward while in attack mode. So also, a bear market slides down on a downward trend. However this slide may be choppy, or fall suddenly like a knife.

In Spain, bull fights are a big sport. In Spain, bull fights are called, "Corrida de toros," that can be literally translated as, "running of the bulls". The Spanish arrived in California in the 16th century. Their culture no doubt influenced America.

In the 19th century (1870s), bulls and bears were baited, by setting vicious dogs upon them. It was part of the main event, which was considered a big cultural event, which was a big Sunday afternoon attraction. This was later banned by the government, citing cruelty to animals.

A good site to read further on Bull and Bear baiting is Atlas Obscura (.com) search for "Bull and Bear fights, California." It has great photos too.

➤ What does a Bullish market signal to traders?

A Bullish market signals a robust, fast moving market, climbing upward, creating a definite "Up-trend."

A bullish market is established when there is a lot of good news in the market, that surges prices of all major stocks collectively. Stocks can climb upward of 10% to 20% and keep climbing higher.

➤ How long can a bull market last?

Traders know the Profit-taking in a bull market is infinite, and stocks can climb up to 50% or higher in just 2 months or in 6 months. History records the longest bull market run is for 3,453 days or 9.46 years, since March 9, 2009.

➤ What does a Bearish market signal to traders?

A Bearish market signals a sluggish, slow moving market, slipping downward, creating a "downtrend."

A bear market is established when stocks slip 20% or more. This is caused due to negative market sentiment and growing pessimism of existing market conditions.

➤ How long can a bear market last?

A short bear market can last between 2 to 4 months, and a Long Bear Market can last up to 1 year and 6 months. Shares can lose up to 40 or 50% of their original value. Recovery can be painful and extremely sluggish. In a bear market, the confidence is low, hovering next to zero, and people panic in bear markets. Many traders assume a "wait and see" position.

➤ What are the Major exchanges that trade stocks?

AMEX - American Stock Exchange.

NASDAQ - National Association of Securities Dealers Automated Quotation System.

MONEY TRADE STOCKS
JACOB DAVID

NYSE - New York Stock Exchange.

➤ What is the S&P 500?

The S&P 500 is an American Index that follows the performance of the top 500 U.S Based, American companies. As of April 30, 2018, the cumulative market capital for the top 500 companies was $23.7 trillion. More importance is given to the strength of capital each of these companies own. To qualify for inclusion in the index, the company must have a minimum of $5.3 Billion capital.

These S&P 500 companies are traded on the NYSE, NASDAQ and CBOE - the Chicago Board Options Exchange.

The S&P 500 index was founded on March 4, 1957. This index measures the stock market's daily/monthly/yearly overall/aggregate performance and the economy's health in one quick view.

Related indices to the 500 are the S&P 1500, S&P Global 1200, S&P 100 stocks.

➤ What are Blue Chip stocks?

Blue Chip stocks are stable stocks with well established capital, efficient management, and good potential for ongoing growth, products, services, and expansion. They have proven track records and are solid in their operations.

Blue chips are a term that comes from the game of poker where the blue chips have the highest value.

➤ Is it safe to invest in Blue Chip stocks?

Yes. 90% of the time, the Blue Chip stocks have a proven track record of growth, indicated by historical growth chart patterns, where over the years, the public have been noticing the growth and expansion of these specific companies.

➤ What is the public sentiment on blue chip stocks?

The public sentiment on these blue chip stocks are usually highly optimistic and positive.

However public sentiment relies on quarterly growth and earnings records, actual facts and figures, not just emotion itself. Public sentiment is cautious during a bear market.

It is advisable not to get emotionally tied or connected to any stock for any reason. As someone once said, "You're trading stock, not getting married to it." So trade without emotion, don't fall in love with a stock. Look for opportunities to make money, increase your net worth.

It is safe to invest in blue chip stocks after you have done your research and studied their history, present financials of the stocks you are interested to invest in.

Generally, with blue chip stocks, traders are usually super conservative and go in for the long term. It is said that Warren Buffett has been holding shares of Coca-cola (KO) for 31 years since 1988, when he bought $1 Billion of the company's shares.

➤ What is the "DOW Jones" ?

MONEY TRADE STOCKS
JACOB DAVID

It is called the DOW Jones Industrial Average (DJIA). This is an index that tracks the top 30 large publicly traded companies on the NYSE and NASDAQ. It covers all the major sectors of the economy, except Transportation and Utilities.

The DJIA index is a "price-weighted" index meaning that the stocks that have higher prices are given more priority over lower priced stocks.

This index also calculates historical data - like stock splits, dividends paid to shareholders, and other changes that happen to the stocks over their life period.

➤ What are the **30 stocks in the DOW Jones' index**? Which year were they added?

3M - MMM - NYSE - 1976
American Express - AXP - NYSE - 1982
Apple - AAPL - NASDAQ - 2015
Boeing - BA - NYSE - 1987
Caterpillar - CAT - NYSE - 1991
Chevron - CVX - NYSE - 2008
Cisco - CSCO - NASDAQ - 2009

MONEY TRADE STOCKS
JACOB DAVID

Coca-Cola - KO - NYSE - 1987
The Walt Disney Co - DIS - NYSE - 1991
Dow DuPont - DWDP - NYSE - 2017
Exxon Mobil - XOM - NYSE - 1928
General Electric - GE - NYSE - 1907
Goldman Sachs - GS - NYSE - 2013
The Home Depot - HD - NYSE - 1999
IBM - IBM - NYSE - 1979
INTEL - INTC - NASDAQ - 1999
JOHNSON & JOHNSON JNJ NYSE - 1997
JP MORGAN CHASE - JPM - NYSE - 1991
McDONALD'S - MCD - NYSE - 1985
MERCK - MRK - NYSE - 1979
MICROSOFT - MSFT - NYSE - 1999
NIKE - NKE - NYSE - 2013
PFIZER - PFE - NYSE - 2004
TRAVELER'S COMPANIES - TRV - NYSE - 2009.
UNITED TECHNOLOGY - UTX NYSE 1939
UNITED HEALTH - UNH - NYSE - 2012
VERIZON - VZ - NYSE - 2004
VISA - V - NYSE - 2013
WAL-MART - WMT - NYSE - 1997

If you are a beginner and are unsure of which companies you'd like to trade, research these top 30 companies, then study the historical patterns of stock movements. Then decide on which stocks you'd like to buy and hold, and for how long.

➤ What times during the day can you trade?

The NYSE - New York Stock Exchange opens at 9.30 AM and closes at 4 PM. Stocks are traded during business days, not on national holidays.

➤ What is the best time to trade stocks?

The best time to trade stocks is from 9.30 to 11:30 (EST) and usually from about 3 PM to 4 PM.

The opening hours of the stock market have more volatility (buoyancy, faster movement) and increased trading (buying & selling) activity than the afternoon session. Each day is different, so I'd suggest watching the market at these different times before you trade.

Before doing actual trades, spend 2 to 4 weeks studying patterns of how fast the market moves, volume of shares traded, and stock chart patterns. Make notes as you learn with daily dates, so you can go back and refer them as needed.

➤ Should I focus on Percentage Earned or Money made when trading stocks?

I would suggest you focus on *Percentage earned*. The secondary part is money made. But while measuring your return on investment, a stronger indicator on returns is percentage, which helps you laser focus on what kind of returns to expect, and this helps you enter and exit the market with fewer distractions and errors.

If you decide to exit after having made 5% on buying a particular stock, then do so. Never get greedy. Do not assume that the stock will keep climbing. If you want to exit after having made a specific percentage, do so.

➤ What is "slippage"?

Slippage in price happens when you miss the price you wanted. If you want to buy or sell a share of ABC stock at $7.10, but instead get it for $7.105 or $7.11 or $7.12, it's because the stock price moves fast, it can get bought or sold at different price, than you originally intended. This is called slippage.

Slippage in price can happen in both directions, both up and down, in buying and selling stock.

➤ How can I avoid "slippage"?

Buy early, before the crowd shows up, or when you have a clear idea by research that the stock is about to do an up-trend.

Second, you can put a "Limit Order" so that if the stock climbs up or goes down, and then comes back to your specific stated price, it will execute your order and buy a set number of shares at that price.

➤ What is the "bid" price?

The bid price is what buyers are willing to pay for a single share of stock.

➤ What is the "ask" price?

MONEY TRADE STOCKS
JACOB DAVID

The ask price is what sellers are willing to take/accept for a single share of stock.

➤ What is the bid-ask spread?

There can be a difference of $0.01 to $0.20 cents between the bid and ask prices of a stock. When there is huge demand for a stock the bid-ask spread can be up to $0.20 cents or more.

➤ How is the bid-ask spread percentage calculated?

If there is a $0.10 cent spread between the BID and ASK prices of the share, divide that by the price of a single share to get the percentage. So if the share price is $25, and there is a difference of $0.10 cents between the Bid and Ask, the bid-ask spread percentage is $0.10 / $25 = 0.004%.

➤ How can you tell if the **trend** is bearish or bullish for a stock without consulting the chart or any of the indicators?

If you wanted to determine the general trend for a stock, up or down, simply compare the previous close price with the present price of the stock (currently trading price) and determine the percentage of uptrend or downtrend.

Second, you can view the heat map for the stock sectors.

➤ What are **Support and Resistance** lines?

Traders of Stock charts rely on Support and Resistance lines to conduct trades. They expect prices to hit Support and Resistance lines and possibly break beyond those lines to set a new trend.

Support and Resistance lines are imaginary lines based on previous historical prices set as early as a week, a few weeks, 1 month, or 3 months. The 3 months historical price may however be outside the scope of today's market conditions, and may not prove accurate. Still it can be used as a point of price reference to gauge the outlook on the market today.

A **Support line** is at the bottom of the trend. It supports the price level from going further down. Previous price levels form the Support line. Traders rely on previous price levels to determine a Support Line. Here's where the bulls start buying and the strength of the stock price is re-stabilized. The bearish trend comes to an end, and a reversal of trend happens. The stock stops going down and starts going back up. In some cases, the bears are so strong that the price breaks below the resistance level and continues going down into more bearish territory. This trend could be uncertain and could continue for a week or two, perhaps even a month. Bearish trends usually last longer than bullish trends. The traders stop trading when the prices are low. Some traders have to wait for the trend to reverse, so they can sell when the stock price climbs back up.

A **Resistance line** is found at the top of the trend. It resists the price of the stock from moving further up. Here, at the resistance line, the bears get active and start selling the stock, thereby weakening price levels. In usual cases, the bears win and the stock price either moves sideways for a few days, or starts dropping down. In some cases, the bulls are so strong that the price breaks through the Resistance line setting a new high. It becomes new land, territory, where the bulls roam free. A new high is when the bulls rage and the stock price climbs up. This trend usually continue a few days. Sometimes it lasts for a few hours.

➤ What is **EBITDA**? (pronounced *Ebit-dah*)

EBITDA is an acronym that means company's Earnings Before Interest, Taxes, Depreciation, and Amortization. This gives you the NET earnings, the true earnings of the company minus all external expenses removed from gross profit. It could also include cost of goods sold. EBITDA is the lean muscle with all the fat and trimmings removed. It shows true financial strength and performance of the company. It could help investors and analysts tremendously to see where the weaknesses in a company's operations may lie.

The EBITDA of the company is used to compare the company's overall financial performance with competitors, sub-sectors, and the overall sector to which it belongs.

Average EBITDA is between 11 and 14, while 10 is seen as above average and healthy by analysts and investors. A negative EBITDA shows that the company is poorly managed or has operational difficulties on the management side. However, investors must be wary of analysis of companies done solely or relying too heavily on EBITDA.

➤ What is **GAAP**?

GAAP is an acronym that is Generally Accepted Accounting Principles. The accountants have to follow set standard principles while calculating final income statements that reveal the true financial strength of the company.

EBITDA and GAAP are commonly used terms on TV channels like CNBC, Bloomberg and shows like Options Action.

➤ What is **P/E ratio**?

This ratio determines how attractive a company is/looks to investors. The ratio measures the current price of the share relative to the earnings per share (EPS). If P/E ratio is absent, and EPS is negative, the company has negative cash flow and could have debt issues. Here are a few examples of companies from different sectors with P/E ratios and EPS.

Apple - AAPL - 24.45x   EPS $11.85
Amazon - AMZN - 83.90x   EPS $22.29
Chipotle - CMG - 78.03x   EPS $10.72
Coca-Cola - KO - 31.34x   EPS $1.77
Exxon - XOM - 20.39x   EPS $3.43
Google - GOOG - 29.47x   EPS $45.97
McDonald's - MCD - 25.90x EPS $7.65
NVIDIA - NVDA - 67.09x   EPS $3.53
Pepsi - PEP - 16.92x   EPS $8.13

➤ What is a **Dividend stock**?

A stock that pays its shareholders a certain sum quarterly, a percentage of their profits, is called a Dividend stock.

When companies do extremely well, these dividend percentage may go up. When companies do poorly, financially, the company can decide to reduce their dividend payments to their shareholders.

Consider dividend payments as "loyalty rewards" for holding the stock. This entices shareholders to not sell the stock, but keep it for longer, because each quarter, the company pays out dividends from its profits. This keeps their shareholders happy.

Example: If a company decides to pay $0.20 cents annually, then if you own 100 shares of ABC stock, it will pay you $0.05 each quarter, which is every 3 months, four times a year. So you would get paid $20 each year for 100 shares.

Not all companies/stocks pay dividends.

➤ What is a "**trailing stop**"?

A trailing stop is also called a trailing stop loss. Usually traders set their trailing stop loss at 15% or 20% below the actual market price of the share. The trailing stop loss adjusts itself as the stock climbs by 15% or 20% as set, but sells when it drops by that much, thereby avoiding huge losses to the trader in the event of a downturn.

➤ What is a **swing low**?

A swing low is when the price of a share drops a few points and then bounces back, starts climbing again.

➤ What is a "**limit order**"?

A limit order is when the trader asks the broker to buy a set of shares at a specific price.

Example: Buy me 100 shares of Coca-Cola Co. (KO) at $49.61, when the stock is trading at or around that price.

This order may or may not buy (execute) based on the stock's volatility, caused by demand and supply created by the stock market.

➤ What is **volatility** in stocks?

Volatility is the range of price change a stock experiences over a period of time, say 1 month, 6 months or 12 months.

A stock is said to have "HIGH volatility" if the price swings rapidly up or down, in a matter of a single day, a few days, or a few weeks.

A stock is said to have "LOW volatility" when the stock price remains stable over a few months, neither going up or down.

A stock's volatility matters a lot for a trader to successfully trade, buy and sell shares of a stock at any given period of time.

A stock with "low volatility" is not going anywhere in a hurry. There is no point of trading such "deadbeat" stocks. You can hardly make any returns on such stocks.

For example: The Energy sector has been in a huge slump since 2016

➤ Why is "stock volatility" important?

MONEY TRADE STOCKS
JACOB DAVID

The range of price movement in stocks can be studied by researching historical charts.

A stock's volatility can be predictable. Traders try to notice such patterns and trade accordingly to make profits on stocks at set times of the year.

➤ What can stock volatility be compared to?

Stock volatility is like the water in the ocean. The stock is the ship that floats on the water (volatility). If there is enough water, the ship floats and gets higher as the water rises. (buoyancy). Inversely, if the water in the ocean gets low, it will run your ship into the rocks.

➤ What is a "Good-till-canceled" (GTC) order?

This means that when you place an order to buy or sell shares and choose "GTC," the order will stay active until you cancel it, or until it gets bought or sold.

➤ What is an IPO?

MONEY TRADE STOCKS
JACOB DAVID

IPO is an acronym that means "Initial Public Offering." This refers to any company that is going public, selling shares to raise capital for operations, for the very first time.

In the case of Levi-Strauss, (LEVI) the blue Denim jeans manufacturer had its first IPO in 1971, then withdrew from the market and went private for 34 years. Then it came back to the NYSE (New York Stock Exchange) market for a second IPO fund raising, on March 21, 2019.

On March 20th, 2019, evening, it decided to release its shares at $17 to the public. However, demand grew and on March 21st, it started trading on the NYSE at $22.22.

➤ Where can I find information about upcoming IPO's?

The NASDAQ website has details of IPO's on its front page, where you could get the Overview, Financials, News Headlines, Experts, just by clicking the links to read information about revenue, net income, liabilities, if the proper documents have all been filed, the date of filing, possible share price range, the exchange where it's going to be traded, outstanding shares, number of employees, CEO name, proposed ticker symbol, company description, competitors, use of proceeds, and other interesting details.

➤ What are some of the things I have to consider before trading an IPO stock?

An IPO stock is an "Initial Public Offering." So check the following items before you trade.

Find out if the company is an American or international company. If it is international, trade tensions can keep the stock IPO from being successful. Traders are a wary bunch, so they keep away from such stocks. In rare instances, they let loose, and trade like crazy.

Find out what the company manufactures, or provides what type of service, how long has the company been in business. Check SEC filings, recent insider trading (buy/sell) if any. Find out what market sector the stock belongs to, and see how popular that sector is.

Find out if the social market sentiment towards the company is positive or negative. Try to put a percentage on the positive and negative view traders have toward the company.

Find out the general and specific news as available on the company. Answer this question, Why is the company going public? Does it want to grow and expand? Does it have positive growth? Or is it looking to raise capital to pay off its debts?

Check to see if there are any red flags regards weaknesses in daily operations, debts and liabilities amassed, new CEO - with or without track record, and anything else negative that may keep traders at bay watching the stock instead of trading it.

Remember IPOs have zero history in the stock market. So each stock will be treading through uncharted, unexplored territory. There are no referral points and traders will be "trading blind". However, you can overcome this by comparing this IPO daily price with well-performing, healthy stocks in the same sector on a daily basis.

Check on possible volume of shares that will be traded on opening day. If you are unsure, wait for a day or two to see where the stock goes in terms of "acceptance" by the public, if the share value rises or falls or stays where it is, going nowhere.

Check if the company will pay any dividends. Check EPS if it is positive or negative, EBITDA if it is positive.

Successful companies have bigger brokers like Morgan Stanley, Goldman Sachs underwriting and issuing the IPO, and valuing the entry price of the stock. Smaller companies cannot afford larger brokers while issuing their IPO.

Remember, with an IPO, never rush in, unless you have done your research and are confident of the sector in general, then of the stock.

Once you are sure of these items, then decide how much you'd like to invest, how many shares of the IPO you'd like to buy, and if you want to hold it long term or for a short term.

MONEY TRADE STOCKS
JACOB DAVID

➤ What is "Paper-trading"?

Paper-trading is practice trading with virtual money. It helps you practice trading on the broker's platform, using their software. This helps you get familiar with the process of buying and selling shares. It helps you understand price movement of the stock, market reaction, sentiment, volatility of the stock, study historical charts, and a host of other aspects, to help you get comfortable with trading stocks.

Always call your broker and talk to their associates about difficulties you find navigating their trading platform. Make notes by dating them, so you can track your learning progress.

Paper trading stocks will help you get comfortable with the trading platform so you can become confident to trade real stocks.

➤ What are Penny stocks?

Penny stocks are priced really low, from $0.001 to $5/- per share. They have the acronym OTC following their ticker symbol, which means "Over the Counter," and is traded through the OTCBB - "Over the Counter Bulletin Board."

Because of their low price, shares of these stocks are often bought in huge quantities by rich investors, who try their best to manipulate the price. When other small investors buy into the stock and the price goes up, then the big investors sell and exit at once. This is called "Pump and dump" of the stock.

Many of the penny stocks over 93% of them are failing companies. They are delisted from major exchanges and sold on unregulated exchanges, and are referred to "Pink Sheets."

Penny stock companies somehow manage to get your mailing address from large data companies. They mail you their brochure telling you that their stock is going to shoot up next month, and ask you to invest in their shares. If you do so, you have a very good chance of making some money. But most likely, if your timing is rotten, you will lose your shirt.

Penny stocks are highly unreliable. The more reliable penny stocks that are serious about making a future for themselves list themselves on the NYSE and NASDAQ exchanges. They slowly outgrow themselves and discard their status of being a "Penny stock," which is looked down upon, as a worthless stock of disrepute.

Penny stocks have been known to on average make 20 - 30% intraday. In unusual cases, penny stocks have jumped up 1400% within a few hours.

➤ What is noticeably different in a Penny stock ticker?

Regular stocks registered on the NYSE, NASDAQ and AMEX have single to four letters. A penny stock has 5 letters.

Example: **RHHBY** - Roche Holding - is a pharmaceutical company based in Basel, Switzerland. Although it's present value is $34.00, it's not registered through the NYSE or NASDAQ or AMEX exchanges.

Check **OTC Markets (.com)** and search RHHBY for details on this stock.

*A company can change its penny stock status anytime by filing with the SEC.

➤ What is .PK and .OB suffix at the end of a stock symbol?

Whenever you see .PK it refers to Pink sheets and .OB refers to Over the Counter Bulletin Board. This is a service provided by the National Association of Securities Dealers (NASD).

➤ What are Pink Sheets?

Pink Sheets is a daily publication compiled by the National Quotation Bureau, with the bid and ask prices of over the counter penny stocks. These stocks are not regulated, nor do they need to meet the minimum requirements set by the Securities Exchange Commission (SEC). This makes all pink sheet stocks highly risky investments. These stocks are volatile and can climb or drop in value in seconds.

However, The NASD Regulation (NASDR) and the Securities Exchange Commission (SEC) regulates market makers in Pink Sheets securities by establishing broad rules that govern their business conduct, qualification standards, check if they meet the legal financial and operational conditions, comply with rules and regulations. Because these are really small companies, it becomes hard to check into their activities at all times.

The NASD and SEC also investigate into alleged violations of securities laws, discipline violators of these regulations, respond to inquiries and complaints from investors and members. There's however no guarantee your complaint will ever get resolved.

Visit **Pink sheets (.com)** for getting more details about pink sheets stocks.

It's always good practice to arm yourself with knowledge, even on penny stocks, so that when the time comes, you can decide on how to act and profit from such knowledge that you have gained. And if you apply your knowledge, and play it right, you can reap untold rewards.

MONEY TRADE STOCKS
JACOB DAVID

➤ What is Intraday trading?

Intraday means all trades that happen the same day, not carrying over to the next day.

Day traders buy and sell shares of stock in anytime before the end of the day. They are allowed 3 intraday trades a week.

Most brokers require a minimum deposit of $25,000 U.S. to become a day trader. This balance in your account removes restrictions allowing you to trade freely.

This amount can be through holdings of stocks in your portfolio.

➤ What is Form SD - Specialized Disclosure Report?

When analyzing a stock for potential to invest, this form SD is included under the SEC filings. This form satisfies Special Disclosure needs implemented under the Dodd Frank Wall Street Reform and Consumer Protection Act relating to conflict minerals in products that companies manufacture. The SD form includes the Conflict Minerals Disclosure Report.

Real Life Example: STMicroelectronics NV is a company based in Switzerland. Ticker Symbol: **STM**, belong to the Information Technology sector, manufactures Semiconductors and Semiconductor Equipment, sources conflict minerals like Gold, Tantalum, Tin, Tungsten which are the core minerals. The SD form discloses these minerals are sourced from countries like China, Indonesia, South Korea, and Thailand. The company employs 253 smelters of different alloys. These suppliers and list of processing facilities are listed in the SD form. Check Stock Ticker **RWLK** ReWalk Robotics, Israel, for an improved SD form.

Now this information can be useful in deciding whether to buy the stock or not. If there is political turmoil in any one of these nations, the supply of these minerals could likely be cut off and STMicroelectronics cannot manufacture its Semiconductors and related equipment.

Arming yourself with this information is crucial before investing in this stock and purchasing its shares. Your decision to buy the shares of

STM should be based on other factors as well, as to how well the company is performing financially, its end customers, debt obligations, assets, liabilities, historical price patterns, EPS, analyst reports, daily average volume traded, upcoming earnings, ex-dividend date, etc. Once you have the full picture, it's time to make your decision.

The whole analysis of this stock should take you about 30 minutes. Make brief notes as you go, if you are seriously considering the stock, for referral purposes at a future date.

Get Mentally Fit

➤ Why must I get mentally fit to become a stock trader?

Stock trading is not just a one day event. If you want to do trading consistently, remember that you have to do it in manageable portions. You can get mentally burned out by having constant exposure to the stock market, facts, figures, charts, and technicals of stocks. It is therefore, important to become mentally fit to become a stock trader.

Mental endurance can be learned through daily practice. Remember to sleep for at least 8 hours daily to keep your mind healthy.

Take 10 minutes a day to learn French, Spanish, or any new language. This will give your mind something new to focus on and get your mind completely off of stocks, renewing your brain by giving it a break from the trading routine.

➤ Why is physical exercise important to becoming a focused trader?

Trading stocks is a sedentary lifestyle. It requires a lot of brain power for analysis, cross checking facts, charts, figures, and numbers, but it keeps you seated for most of the day. Remember to eat on time, go to sleep on time. Physical exercise can include stretching daily in between trading, doing pushups, sit ups, if your back is strong, early walks for 30 minutes once in two days at least. Walking is sufficient if you have physical limitations. Getting up early by 6:00 AM actually allows you to plan your day and become effective at trading.

Remember to breathe in plenty of fresh air, it's free after all, yet people don't breathe in fresh air. Inhale, hold for 5 to 10 seconds, Exhale. Make it a point not to think of trading during your walks. Take time to interact with nature and God as you walk. This allows you to empty your mind and think on spiritual things, which keeps your mind healthy and alive, gets it ready for the day.

➤ Why must I follow a schedule to trade?

The stock market follows a schedule, so too, you must follow a schedule if you want to be serious about trading, for the single reason of making money. Building Discipline is key.

TECHNICALS:

It is important to learn about technical analysis of stocks to gauge the direction the market is going to take. It informs you as a trader.

Learning how to set these charts and understanding the reason behind them is of crucial importance. Your broker can help you set these charts up.

When analyzing stock technical charts, it is important not to rely on just any one chart. Rather it is advisable to consult a few charts before you make an informed decision to buy or sell the stock.

MACD Indicator. (Mack-Dee)
Stochastic Momentum Index.
RSI - Relative Strength Index.

There are a host of other studies, which you could learn about and set up to inform each purchase or sale. First learn these 3 indicators before you proceed to set up others.

➤ What is a **MACD** Indicator? What are the settings for this?

A MACD (pronounced *Mack Dee*) line indicator was developed by Gerald Appel in the 70's. MACD stands for "Moving Average Convergence / Divergence" oscillator.

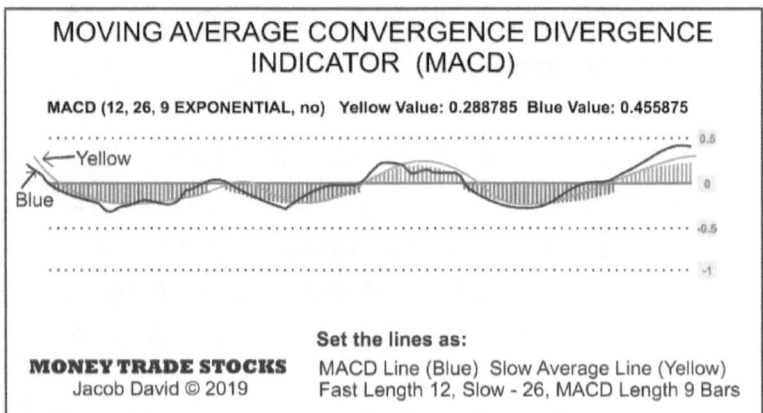

It is one of the most easy to read indicators out there. It follows the trend and the momentum of the stock, the speed at which shares are being traded.

The MACD line fluctuates and trades below and above the center line 0.0 with -0.5 under it and 0.5 above the zero.

Investors use the MACD indicator to identify the right time to buy or sell, based on the crossover of the BLUE MACD line over the YELLOW slow moving average of the 12 and 26 days.

The two lines converge, then crossover and diverge, the MACD line going above the moving average line, signalling an up or down trend. However, the MACD does not show "overbought" and "oversold" positions for any stock.

➤ What are the typical settings traders choose for the **MACD** indicator?

12, 26 and 9 are typically chosen while setting the MACD indicator/chart.

Baseline = Value "0" and has the color purple. You can give this line any other color.

The MACD line is the 12 day **Exponential Moving Average** (EMA) minus the 26 day EMA.

Fast Length = 12 day moving average.

Slow Length = 26 day slow moving average.

Signal Line = Fast 9 day moving average, EMA of MACD line. BLUE Line.

Slow Average Line - Yellow.

MACD Histogram = MACD line - Signal line.

MACD Line = 12 day EMA - 26 day EMA

➤ What is the "**Accumulation Distribution Indicator**"?

The Accumulation Distribution is a technical indicator created by Dominico D'Errico. It is designed to measure the Demand and Supply for stocks.

Accumulation is when the line goes up signaling that traders are buying stocks.

Distribution is when the line goes down signaling that the traders are selling stocks. There is the "overbought" condition when the trend starts a reversal and starts going downward. There is the "oversold" condition when the trend starts a reversal and starts climbing upward.

➤ What does the **Accumulation Distribution Indicator** study?

The Accumulation Distribution indicator compares current share price with past values.

MONEY TRADE STOCKS
JACOB DAVID

There are two levels at which the price is calculated - the high-low range and the average true range.

The study has two plots - the Range Ratio and the Range Factor, which helps the indicator to work. The Range ratio studies the high-low current range of price or the average true range comparing it to a past value of that range, which is expressed in percent.

The Range factor is a reference line for the Range ratio plot.

Inputs: Length = 4, Factor 0.75, Mode: Range. Drawing can be set as a line or candles, whichever visually appeals to you. You can consult with your broker to change these settings.

If the Accumulation Distribution graph candles/line cross the value of 1.0, it signals that the buyers are ready to accumulate (buy) shares.

Usually the graph starts at 0 to 3, and above 0.75 signals a trend change for the better, going upward. This graph can change upwards from 0 to 20 or more even, if stock price gets aggressive and moves up really fast.

Example: ELTK - Eltek Ltd Com, an Information Technology company based in Israel, a small cap value industry, had its stock price shoot from 1.64 previous close to $7.00 end of next day. The day's change was +$5.36 (upward 326.83%). Example as of May 29, 2019 (date for chart referral purposes).

The Accumulation Distribution graph shot up to 15.85 range ratio, trading a total of 36,192,930 shares through the day. This is not an everyday happening. Quite unusual.

➤ What is the **Relative Strength Index** (RSI) indicator?

The Relative Strength Index indicator was developed by J. Welles Wilder Jr. which was explained in his book, "New Concepts in Technical Trading Systems," (1978). The RSI measures the collective range of recent price changes to indicate overbought or oversold conditions.

The relative strength index oscillates between zero and one hundred. When the RSI is above 70, it signals an overbought condition, and when the RSI is below 30 it signals an oversold condition. Because of this, RSI is used to signal the general trend of the stock - upward or down.

In a **Bull market**, the RSI stays between the range of 40 and 90 where 40 and 50 acts as the (lower) support range. When the index line crosses 70, traders get ready for a reversal downward trend to take place. The stock enters the overbought territory and a downward trend reversal could start at any time.

In a **Bear market**, the RSI stays between 10 and 55 range, with the 50 and 60 range acting as the (higher) resistance area. When the index line crosses the 30 mark, traders get ready for an upward trend reversal to take place. The stock enters the oversold territory and an upward trend reversal could start at any time.

The RSI indicator does a good job of informing traders of the market trade conditions.

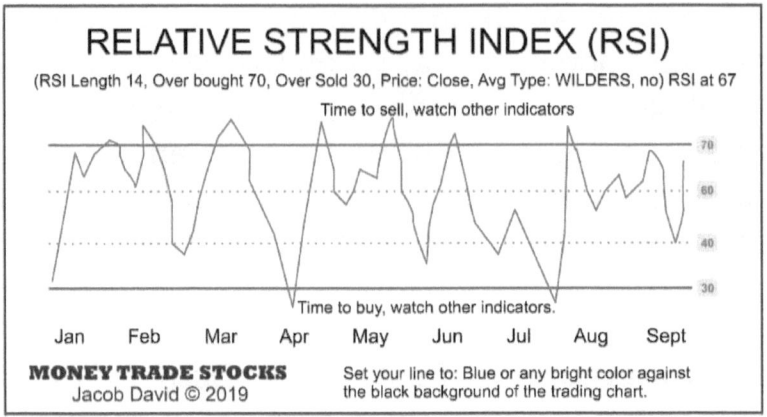

The Rate of Change (ROC) momentum oscillator focuses only on upward or downward momentum. It is related to the RSI.

➤ How to set the **RSI** study:

Click set studies, search for RSI and click it. Open the panel and set the parameters.

Set the RSI Length to 14 bars, each bar representing one trading day, for the past 14 days.

Set the Overbought number to 70. Some people set this to 80 to allow some more room to exit the market. However, keeping the original settings is highly recommended.

Set the Oversold number to 30.

The Relative Strength Index charts the current and historical strength or weakness of a stock based on the closing prices of a recent trading period.

➤ What is the **Stochastic Momentum Index**? (SMI)

The Stochastic Momentum Index takes into account a range of historical prices **relative to the midpoint** of the most recent high to low range of prices. It focuses on this midpoint price range to guess the next trend of the stock, if the stock price will go on an uptrend or head on a downtrend. (The actual definition has been simplified by me, as it's way more twisted and complicated).

The Stochastic Momentum Index is an improvement on the traditional stochastic oscillator, developed by William Blau in 1993.

The oscillator or the SMI index defines clearly the overbought or oversold conditions for the stock being researched. However, it would do good for the trader not to solely rely on the SMI chart alone, to make his/her decision.

➤ Input Settings for the SMI:

Overbought condition set at +40. Red color.

Oversold condition set at -40. Green color.

Percent of d length = 3 (the number of bars used to smooth the SMI).

Percent of k length = 5 (the number of bars used to calculate the SMI).

Remember not to rely on the SMI chart alone.

How to read the Stochastic Momentum Index:
Crossover 1: SMI passes moving average from below signals a BUY once it goes above -40.

Crossover 2: SMI falls below the moving average line from above signals a SELL +40, on it's way downward.

Crossovers that hang around between the -15 to +15 ranges are often seen as unreliable by traders.

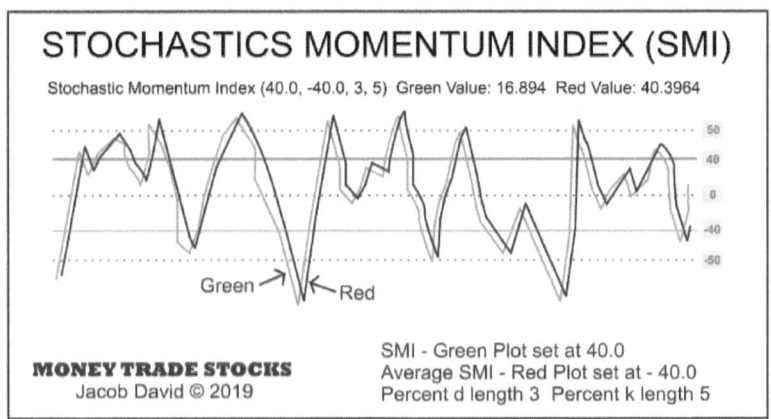

Remember, If the trend is not strong, volatility is absent, and there is no clear direction for the day, either upward or downward, this signal suggests that you don't make your trade for the day. (The above graph is for illustrative purposes only).

➤ What studies do I need to add to the **Price chart**?

Set up "Simple Moving Averages" and "Exponential Moving Averages" to the Price chart. These lines give visual suggestions as to the nature of the stock market sentiment, over the last 20 days, 50 days, and over 200 days.

Simple Moving Average (Close, 20, 0, no)
Price = To Close.
Length = 20, Give Color Blue.
Displace = 0.
Show breakout signals = No.

Simple Moving Average (Close, 50, 0, no)
Price = To Close.
Length = 50, Give Color Orange.
Displace = 0.
Show breakout signals = No.

Simple Moving Average (Close, 200, 0, no)
Price = To Close.
Length = 200, Give Color Yellow.
Displace = 0.
Show breakout signals = No.

Moving Average Two lines (Set this up)
(Close, 3, 8, 0, Exponential)
Price = To Close.
Fast Length = 3, Give Color Purple.
Slow Length = 8, Give Color Green.
Displacement = 0.
Average Type = Exponential.

MONEY TRADE STOCKS
JACOB DAVID

The Exponential moving averages of **3** and **8** show how these lines converge and cross over then diverge to give traders **clear signals** as to **which direction** the market is headed.

When the **EMA's Purple 3** converges over the **EMA's Green 8**, and diverges, it's a **Buy Signal**, an upward trend, and vice versa.

➤ What signals a reversal of the bearish trend?

A bearish trend can be short or long. A lot of variables other than the chart go into the reversal of a bearish trend.

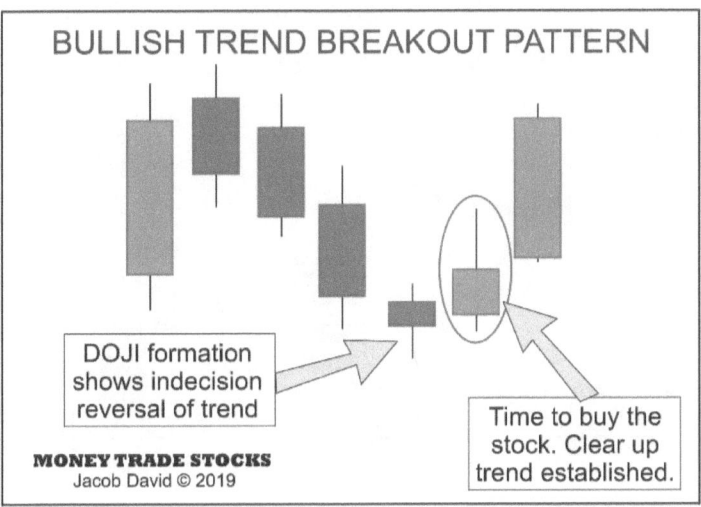

The stock chart shows a DOJI or a hammer head, which shows indecision, followed by a higher green candle, that signals a buy pattern, traders going in to buy, accumulate shares of the stock.

This usually sets the trend in an upward direction. However, it is necessary to watch the chart for a strong bullish push upward, before purchasing the stock.

➤ What signals a reversal of a bullish trend?

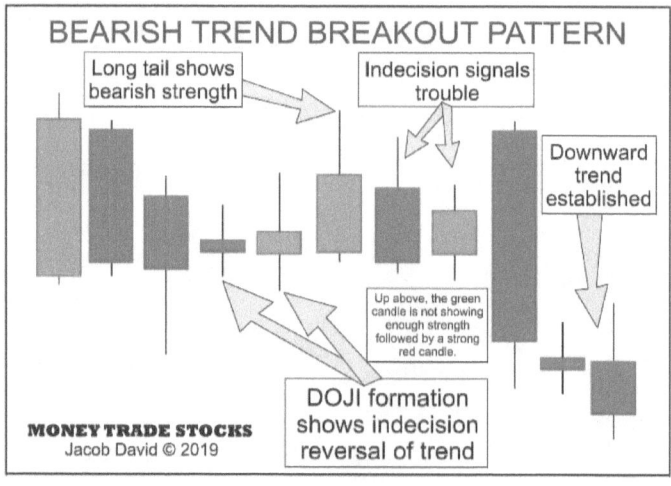

Sometimes a stock can go sideways for a while, before a bearish trend begins. After a bullish trend, indecision on the part of traders can make the stock go sideways.

This can be followed by alternate green and red candles. A Doji candle does not have to appear every time, as you will see.

Weaker green candles with longer tails, the green resting heavier on the bottom signals a downward trend. This shows the bears pushing downward.

CANDLESTICK CHARTING:

➤ How did Candlestick charts come to be?

Candlestick charts were gifted to the world by the Japanese rice traders. It's supposed that Munehisa Homma, a rice trader from Sakata, Japan, developed the method of candlestick charting as early as 1750, in the 18th century. This knowledge was then studied and spread to the Western world by Steve Nison, in his book, "Japanese Candlestick Charting Techniques."

➤ Why is it called a Candlestick?

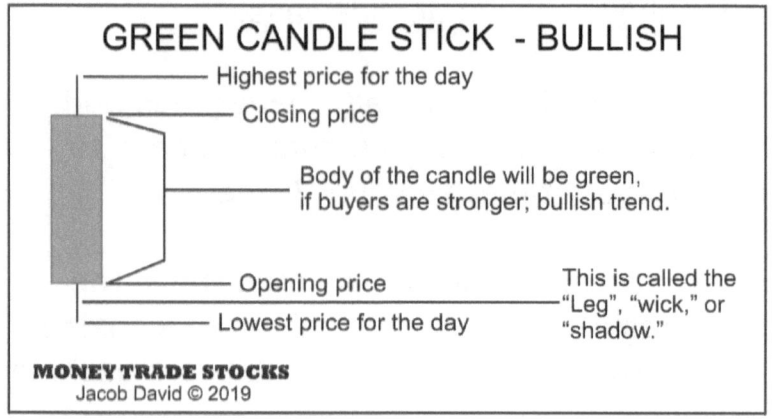

The chart displays green and red shaped bars that are shaped like Candlestick. The green candle displays a "bullish trend," which suggests that buyers are buying shares. The red candle displays a "bearish trend" which suggests that the sellers are strong and are selling shares.

The green or red candle may or may not have wicks on both ends. It's called a "wick," "leg," "tail," or "shadow." If it does not have a "tail" or "wick" then it's called a shaven candle.

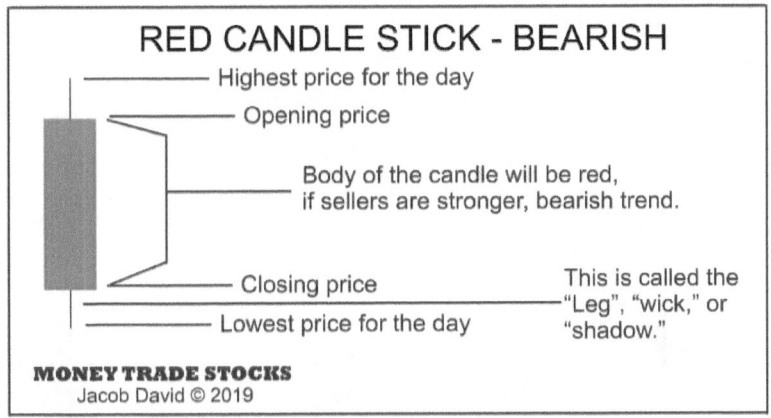

For a red candle, the **only difference** is that the price opens at the top and closes at the bottom of the candlestick.

The body of the candle displays the prevailing psychology of the traders reflecting the current trend in the market.

➤ What are some common candlestick patterns?

Some of the common candlestick patterns are:

1. Hammer
2. Hanging man
3. Doji
4. Bearish engulfing and Bullish engulfing
5. Bullish Harami

6. Shooting star

A **Hammer candlestick** and **The Hanging Man** candlestick patterns have small bodies with long legs or lower shadows. The smaller bodies are at the top.

The candle is shaped like a hammer head. Usually the Hammer candlestick is found at the base of a down trend, meant to be hammering out a base.

A **Doji** forms when there is indecision in the market. Neither the bulls or bears are dominant or triumphant.

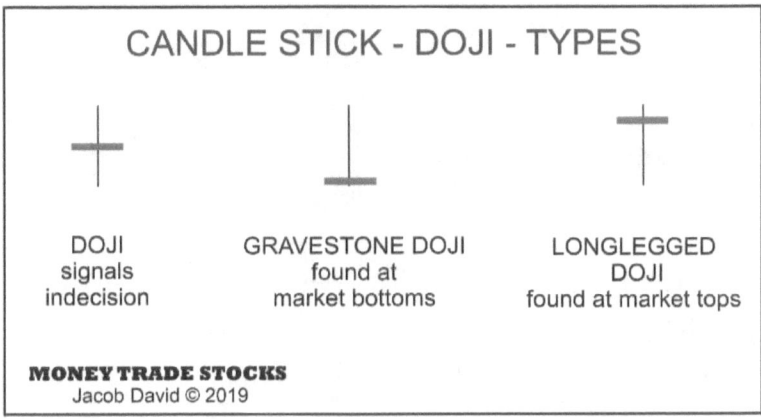

The **Gravestone Doji** usually forms at the bottom of the market. It is shaped like a gravestone, with a base and a top.

The **Long-legged Doji** often appears at the top of a market. This means the up trend has lost its steam, and traders are facing the dilemma of having "non-direction." **The Dragonfly** is the opposite of a Gravestone Doji.

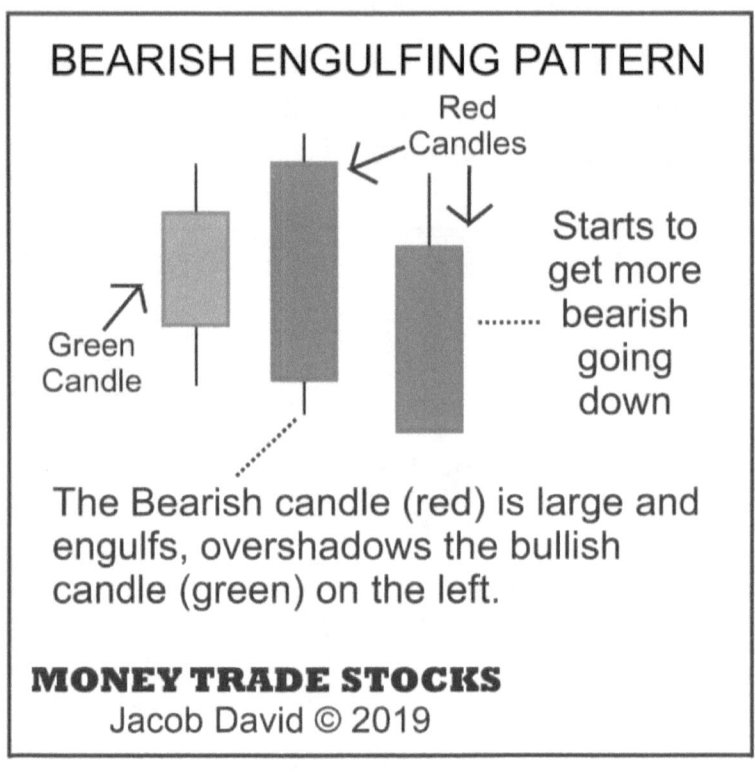

The Bearish Engulfing candlestick pattern is formed at the end of a bullish trend.

The green candle is engulfed by a bearish red candle to its right, which signals a reversal in trend, usually to the downside, the beginning of a downtrend.

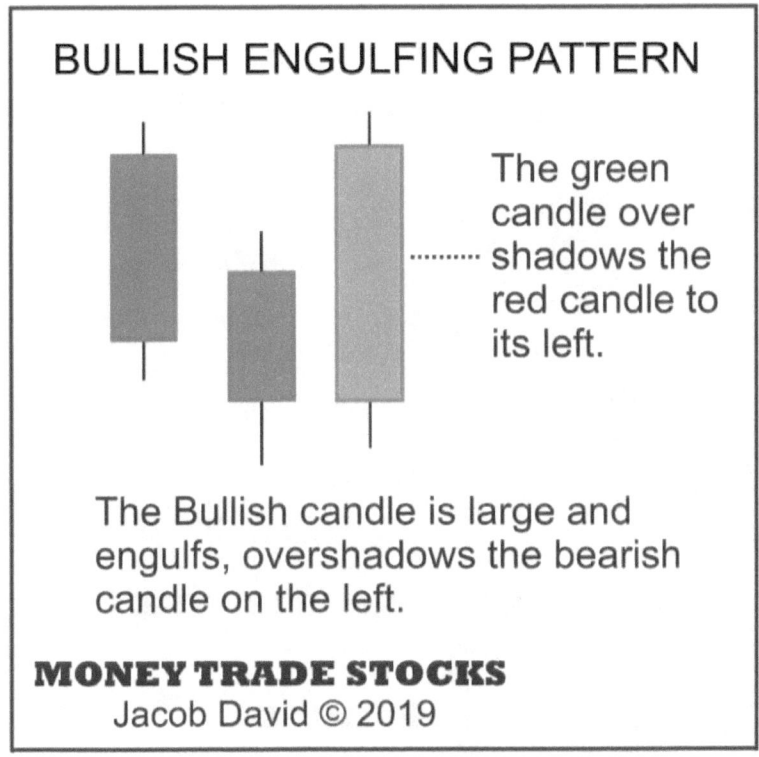

The **Bullish Engulfing** pattern forms at the end of a bearish trend.

A large green candle forms, engulfing the red bearish candle to its left. This suggests the beginning of an upward, bullish trend.

The Bullish Harami candlestick pattern is formed after a heavy bearish trend.

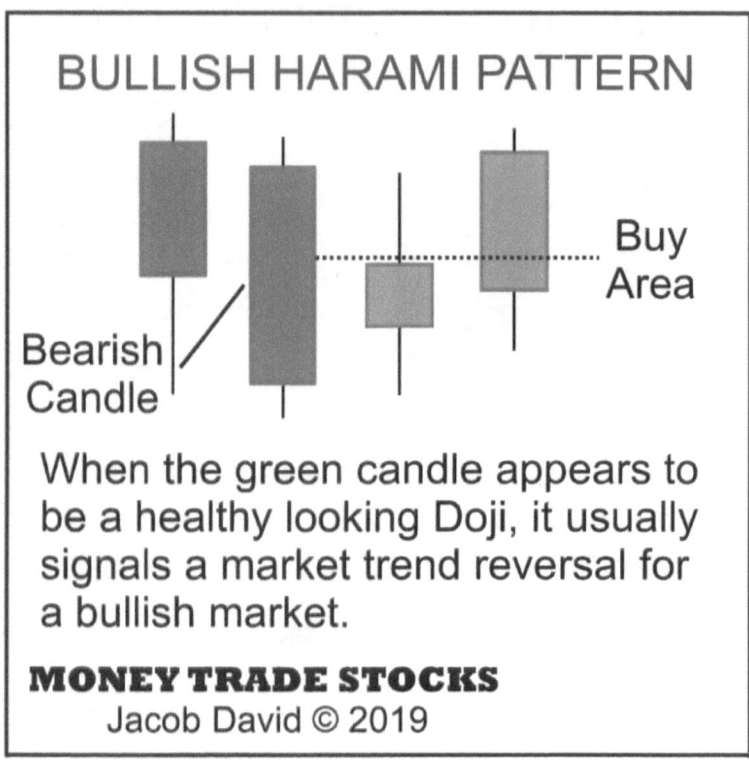

The chart candles show the formation of a green candle that suggests that a reversal of trend may be happening, the onset of a bullish upward trend.

In some cases, the small green Doji, could be grayed out or white.

Each candle in the chart below represents one trading day. Two red candles show two bearish days, and one green candle on the third day shows a reversal in trend, signaling an upward trend.

A healthy Doji is formed and this usually signals a reversal of the bearish trend, the start of a bullish market, upward trend.

A **Shooting Star** candlestick pattern is an upside down hammer. If it is found at the top of a bullish trend, then it signals that a reversal is possibly coming.

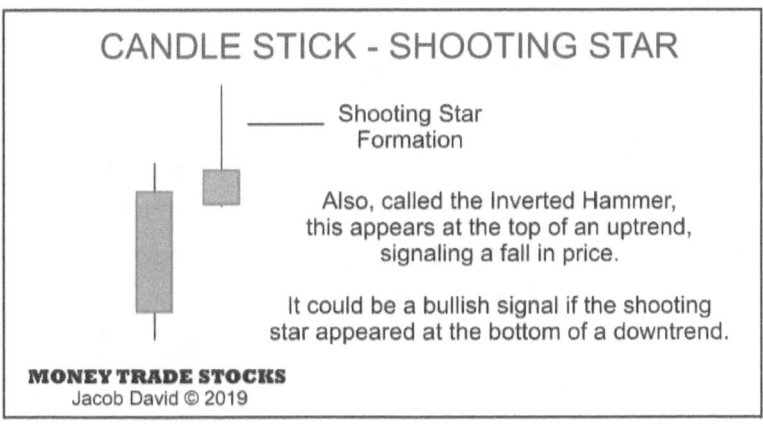

If it is found at the bottom of a bearish trend, then the Shooting Star is a bullish signal.

However, it is important that you wait for an uptrend to happen, before you place a trade.

➤ Where could the **DOJI** possibly have got its name?

The Doji could most likely have got its name from the Dojima Rice Exchange, called the Dojima kome ichiba, located in Osaka, Japan, possibly established around 1697. By 1710, the exchange got into trading of futures and lasted until 1939, when the Government Rice Agency took over. For nearly 200 years, the Dojima Rice Exchange took care of business, handling over 1300 rice dealers.

➤ What is **DRIP** investing?

DRIP is an acronym that stands for Dividend Reinvestment Plan. The money that the trader receives from a dividend stock is accumulated and reinvested into the same stock, purchasing more shares of the stock. This is a slow process but effective when the money adds up and buys an extra share or two, which in turn gets you additional dividend, increasing your earnings. It is a great way to put all of your money to work in an efficient way. To get this DRIP started, contact your broker who can help you get this set up.

➤ What are **ETFs**?

ETFs is an acronym for "Exchange Traded Funds." They are many stocks held in one basket. An ETF mitigates the market risk for the trader versus holding just one stock.

An ETF normally owns hundreds or thousands of domestic or international stocks across various sectors or industries. Some funds focus on stocks on a global level.

The **different types of ETFs** are:

1. Industry specific ETFs.
2. Commodity specific ETFs.
3. Currency specific ETFs.
4. Bond ETFs.
5. Inverse ETFs which gains value when the share's price loses value.

➤ Are all ETFs commission free?

Some ETFs are commission free, while others have low expense ratios and fewer broker low fee/expense commissions to buy or sell them.

Checklist before buying any stock:

➤ What must I do before placing a trade?

You can never be too careful before placing a trade. Afterall, you are getting ready to invest your money into a stock and buy its shares, thereby getting a share of ownership in the company because you believe in it. There are multiple things you can check for before you buy the stock.

Make sure the ticker symbol is right. Some people miss it by a single letter and end up buying some other stock. This happens if the trader is over confident or just plain careless.

Make sure the stock is reversing its trend to an upward trend.

It should have made a climb of 3 to 5% earnings as the day starts or pre-market, and you can see it's climbing up steadily.

Make sure there is a good demand and supply of at least 500,000 shares to 100 Million shares are being traded. Check the stock chart for this number. It is usually found in the left corner of your stock chart.

Make sure the stock chart has the study for Simple Moving Average (SMA) 3 days line and the 8 days line, Exponential Moving average (EMA) set up. You can give the 3 day SMA a purple color and the 8 day EMA to dark green color. Make sure the purple line converges with the dark green line and crosses over the green line. This signals a buying trend and an upward climb. (You can always call your broker for assistance to help set this up).

Check the MACD line and make sure that the line has converged and crossed over the Signal line to show a clear upward trend.

Check the "Accumulation Distribution Indicator" that measures underlying market supply and demand. The lines depict if traders are accumulating (buying) or distributing (selling) stocks.

Glance at the RSI - Relative Strength Indicator to see the overbought or oversold conditions. If it is not clear, do some more research.

Check the "Time and Sales" Column on the right of your stock price chart, which signals how many shares of the specific stock are being bought and sold in real-time.

➤ What other aspects must I **Quick Check** about a stock before buying that stock?

If you are analyzing a new stock for the first time, check these things:

The share's current price. Usually if the price stays a consistent green color, it shows the stock is steadily climbing upward. If the color keeps flickering between green and red, it shows the market is indecisive. Try not to trade on that day. **Check the following:**

"Market Cap." If the market cap is above 500M, it stands a good chance as a stable company. Check the annual report to see active debts or loans.

Outstanding shares. Shares in excess of 500M could mean too much supply of shares, and could lead to low demand. Example BAC Bank of America has 9.5 Billion shares outstanding. Hence their share price value has stayed between $22 and $30/- for nearly 3 years.

Dividends paid, if any. Percentage of dividends.

Calculate the percentage of dividend, compare with the price of the stock in terms of returns.

"52 week range," high and low, gives you an idea of how strong the stock is, relative to price.

EPS - "Earnings per share," if positive or negative.

"Historical volatility" - check this if the number is above 60% then the stock price can change value rapidly. Below 60% is somewhat more conservative in price fluctuations.

Check "Held by institutions" - if this is above 50 and less than 70% is a good area. If it is over 70% then too many institutions own it and the stock may as a result be sluggish.

Read today's "News" about the stock. Read the answer to what is a "Catalyst"? to see how news can affect the price of the stock.

Check "**Short interest**" which reveals what percentage of traders try to short the stock and a possible range in percentage of shorts held, those that are floating short and active currently. TSLA Tesla has a short interest of 28.12% as float since 5/15/19 while Beyond Meat BYND has a short interest of 7.15% since 5/15/19.

Quickly scan **SEC filings**, check if there are any insider trades, especially suggesting confidence, if the Board of Directors have purchased shares at a specific price or granted shares at "0" value, as part of their hire package. Code "A" for acquired shares.

Similarly check for **insider trades** can suggest low confidence if the Board of Directors have sold shares, code "D" for disposed off shares. This could mean the stock is in trouble in the near future, up ahead.

Check if there are any upcoming "Dividends" or "Earning announcements. This can affect the trend of the stock price drastically. Use a stock screener to isolate stocks that have Earnings announcements coming up in the next week. Also, do a study of how prices fluctuate for different stocks around Earnings Announcements season.

➤ What is **EPS** for a stock?

EPS stands for Earnings Per Share for a stock. The profit of the company is divided by the outstanding number of shares to get the Earnings Per Share. The company is considered to be more profitable if it has a higher EPS.

Formula for calculating EPS:

Net Income - Preferred Dividends
Common shares outstanding
(at end of period)

The strength of the EPS is a good and reliable indicator that can help you to pick good stocks. EPS shows how much money is made for each share of the stock, which shows how financially strong the company is. While this book gives you the general idea of what the EPS is and how it is calculated, there are other complex methods to calculate the Diluted EPS and EPS from continuing operations.

➤ What is included in an **Earnings report**?

Earnings report includes the quarter's revenue, expenses, and net profit along with other details which every company files with the Securities Exchange Commission (SEC) using a 10 Q form. This helps shareholders and the public (potential future shareholders) come to know of the company's financial performance.

➤ What are **Estimates**, **Beat**, and **Miss**?

It is the job of Wall Street analysts to analyze various company stocks, and predict company performance based on previous quarter financials, present day debt holdings, potential for new products and services, and crunching various factors to predict how well a company will perform in the upcoming quarter. These are called Estimates of Performance.

If the actual earnings numbers beats Analysts' estimates, the share prices will shoot up.

If the actual earnings' numbers misses Analysts' estimates, the share prices will fall, thereby devaluing the stock price.

➤ What is **Guidance**?

Most companies provide an estimate report on where they see the company going in the next quarter and upcoming year. This is called Guidance. They are not required to do this. However, reputable and well meaning, ethical companies provide shareholders with enough transparency as to what the public can expect in the upcoming months and the next few years. It lays out a plan of expansion and growth and vice versa, where the company foresees challenges or difficulties based on market conditions. Stock prices can rise or fall based on the content in this Guidance release.

➤ What is the **P/E ratio**? (Additional info).

The P/E ratio is used to calculate if the stock is overvalued or undervalued. The P/E ratio is calculated by dividing the company's current share price by the company's earnings per share.

The P/E ratio historical average range has been between 15 - 25. A stock's P/E tells us how much traders are willing to pay per dollar of earnings.

A negative P/E ratio means the stock is not doing so well, and by extension, the company is having losses and negative earnings per share.

➤ What are the **Lows and Highs** for a stock?

The low amount and high amount that a stock touches during the year becomes the historical high and low for the stock, for that year.

The lows and highs gives you the entire range.
What are earnings announcements?

An "Earnings announcement" is an official public statement released that indicates how well a company has done for that quarter or annually.

Analysts study stocks are come up with estimates of possible earnings. If the official earnings beats analysts' estimates, then the stock price will soar, and vice versa.

The NASDAQ website has an earnings calendar. Yahoo Finance website also has an earnings calendar. (Remember to google and bookmark these pages). Consult them daily or as often as you can.

➤ What is a **Stock Screener**?

A stock screener helps you narrow down on stocks based on several criteria - price and volume, sector, market capital, dividends, technicals, analyst ratings, performance, and stock fundamentals to name just a few. This helps you arrive at top performing stocks OR top stocks that have lost value in just the last day or so.

➤ Why should I take profits and rearrange my portfolio regularly?

MONEY TRADE STOCKS
JACOB DAVID

Taking profits periodically is the best way to grow your income. Never grow complacent or disinterested. If you grow disinterested, take a break for a few weeks and come back.

Meanwhile, keep an eye on existing stocks in your portfolio, while on your break. Do not leave your portfolio ignored.

Here's why it is good to take profits regularly.

Example: If you have $6,000 to buy AAPL shares trading at $179.83, then you can buy 33 shares before commissions. Apple pays dividends of 1.72% annually or $3.08 per share ($0.77 cents every quarter). That would be 33 shares x $3.08 = $101.64 yearly earnings in dividends, if you hold the share for a full year.

Two months pass by and the share price climbs up to $215.36 per share. Now the difference in increase in share value is $35.53 per share.

Total earnings is $35.53 x 33 shares = $1172.49. It's better than the dividend earned on 33 shares each year.

MONEY TRADE STOCKS
JACOB DAVID

Profit Percentage = $1172.49/$6,000 which was your original investment, equals to 19.5% return in just 2 months. That is 9.7% return each month.

So, if you sell now, keeping a 20% return in mind, and you are at 19.5% you must be flexible to exit the trade.

So you exit and take a decent profit of $1172.49 and you get your $6,000 back into your account as well, for a total of $7172.49.

Now let's say your friend decides to stick it out a little longer and hold AAPL stock, hoping it will climb further. The profile of APPLE stock shows that year high has been $233.47 and so he hopes it will climb higher. He crosses his fingers and waits anxiously.

The following Tuesday there is a sudden increase in global trade tensions between America and China. This causes the Apple stock to drop drastically at 7% per day, for 3 to 4 days, erratic drops, down to 23% drop total for a final share price of $165.83. Now your friend is stuck, unable to sell his shares.

Neither did he have the chance to take any profits.

Now Apple stock (AAPL) has fallen down $14 per share, from his original purchase price of $179.83/- That is a - 8.8% loss from his purchase price. Now his 33 shares are valued at $5472.39 which is a loss of -$527.61.

Now your friend may have to hold the Apple stock another 3 months to 6 months before the stock can climb back to $215/-.

Nothing is certain in the stock market. If the trade tensions get worse between American and China, the stock price for Apple could drop further, causing him a lot of heartache and pain, not counting the financial loss, waiting time, and the misery he experiences in the process.

This is why it's advisable to **keep an EXIT strategy via percentage earnings**. Once you have reached a certain percentage of positive earnings, take your profit and your original balance back to your account.

Now you, being the smart investor, unlike your friend are READY to buy Apple stock for a second trade round.

You start watching the AAPL stock ticker daily to see the news and if the global trade tensions have receded. This would help you to decide if you want to re-invest in Apple, once it starts climbing again. You buy Apple stock once it confirms an up trend and buy for $6,000 again. Perhaps you can use a part of your profits up to $250/- or $500/- which is being aggressive. So now you can buy 3 more additional shares for the added $500, up to 36 shares, spending a total of $6,500.

You wait for the Apple stock to climb up to $215 or close to $215 and sell again, a profit of $1,240/- which is a 19% profit a second time.

Now, remember that you have to watch your Apple stock closely, everyday, along with the news. Make sure you are ready to sell even at 10% or 12% if the market suddenly turns downward. Don't get sad. Always remember you are at least taking a 10% profit. **Never get greedy!** That's a good lesson to remember while trading. Write in your evening notes that you made 10% on **AAPL** for that day.

As of **1/3/2020**, AAPL is now at $300.204¢. Apple stock climbed from a low of $142 on **Jan 3, 2019** to a high of $300.20 on **Jan 3, 2020**, a 112% increase. (**Profit per share** $158.20).

➤ What is **short-selling** of a stock?

Traders are allowed to borrow shares of the particular stock from someone or the broker and sell them, speculating that the market price for that stock will fall. When the price falls, they buy it back at the low price, making a profit, and exiting their position. They return the stock back to the lender after having made a profit. Such trading is called short selling, and these traders are called short-sellers.

➤ How does short-selling affect the market?

Short-selling is a legal activity allowed by the SEC. The trader takes a negative position on the stock, predicting and wishing for the stock to fall in price. If a horde of traders do this all at once, they effectively manipulate the stock sending it into a bearish tailspin, bringing down the stock price down drastically. Market sentiment based on company news, events, and a host of factors lead to shorting a stock.

➤ What is a short-Sale restriction?

In February 2010, the SEC adopted the price restriction. It is commonly referred to "the alternative uptick rule, (Rule 201)." The "circuit-breaker" prevents short sellers from driving down prices further down, if the stock has already lost 10% for the day, compared to the closing price for the previous day. This rule applies to all stocks listed on all the national securities exchange or over the counter markets.

➤ Why did the SEC approve the Short-Sale restriction?

The SEC approved the short-sale restriction to keep investor confidence in the stock up. It also did not want the stock price to plunge excessively due to short-selling, promoting market greed. This short-sale price fall is artificially created by investor speculation. It is not created by natural market events like bad news or bad performance related to that specific company.

To read more on the restriction, visit this link: https://www.sec.gov/news/press/2010/2010-26.htm

➤ What are some **top stocks under $10**?

These five are based on a stock screener dated June 5, 2019. Your input into the stock screener can be different and you may get a different list. These stocks will provide you a start. Look at these stocks in some detail, to see if they are worth investing into.

CAMT - Camtek Ltd - $8.38 pays no dividend.

SECO - Seco Holdings - $7.49 pays no dividend.

SCX - L S Starrett Co - $6.95 pays no dividend.

SLM - SLM Corp - $9.98 pays 1.20% dividend.

MONEY TRADE STOCKS
JACOB DAVID

SVBI - Severn Bancorp - $8.60 pays 1.40% dividend.

Invest in these stocks, if you feel confident.

➤ What are some **top stocks under $20**?

AMRB - American River Bankshares - $12.08 pays 1.66% dividend.

BT - BT Group PLC - $13.28 pays 7.52% dividend.

CFBK - Central Federal Corp - $12.42 pays no dividend.

CTRN - Citi Trends Inc - $13.67 pays 2.34% dividend.

FCCY - 1st Constitution Bancorp - $18.77 pays 1.60% dividend.

HZO - MarineMax Inc - $15.90 pays no dividend.

LMST - Limestone Bancorp Inc - $15.02 pays no dividend.

MONEY TRADE STOCKS
JACOB DAVID

PUMP - ProPetro Holdings - $18.28 pays no dividend.

TTM - Tata Motors - $12.50 pays no dividend.

UBNK - United Financial Bancorp - $13.48 pays 3.65% dividend.

Research these stocks and historical chart patterns before you invest in them. Study current news and SEC filings on these companies. (This list as of June 5, 2019)

➤ What are some **top stocks under $50**?

BK - Bank of New York Mellon - $43.61 pays 2.57% dividend.

DHI - D.R. Horton Homes - $44.63 pays 1.34% dividend.

EV - Eaton Vance Group - $39.68 pays 3.53% dividend.

FANH - Fanhua Inc $31.51 pays 3.33% dividend.

MONEY TRADE STOCKS
JACOB DAVID

FBK - FB Financial Corp - $35.78 pays 0.89% dividend.

PPL - PPL Corp - $31.15 pays 5.30% dividend.

PUK - Prudential PLC - $41.21 pays 3.16% dividend.

SLF - Sun Life Financial - $39.92 pays 3.90% dividend.

TOL - Toll Brothers - $36.49 pays 1.21% dividend.

WRK - Westrock Co - $35.88 pays 5.07% dividend.

Check if these stocks will tank due to global trade tensions. Research into where these companies get their raw materials from, and how they react to global tensions.

➤ What are **ADR Fees**?

ADR (American Depository Receipt) fees are normally charged for foreign stock. If you are interested in buying stocks of companies in China, India, and other countries, these fees plus other fees may apply.

ADR fees are charged by custodial banks of the stocks which normally average from 1 to 3 cents per share. Other country fees might apply. So make sure of what extra fees apply before you buy those stocks.

Some examples of foreign stocks that have ADR fees are: TTM - Tata Motors (India), NIO - Nio Electric Corp, and BILI - Bili Bili (China).

➤ How do I start trading?

Trading requires preparation. It requires knowledge of ONLY the sectors of the market YOU are interested in. Also, make sure that the sectors you are interested in can actually make you money. DO NOT get interested in a sector because a friend or family member used to work in that sector 20 years ago.

Remember this always: The stock market is emotionless, money is without emotion, and your trades must be without emotion, purely based on charts, stock news, and trends.

➤ Should I trade daily?
You can trade daily ONLY if there are good opportunities to do so. Don't go chasing stock prices, or trends. You must have a legitimate reason to trade. Remember you are buying stock because the market has given you a reason to do so. The same goes for selling a stock to exit the position, or to "short" a stock. **Don't trade** a stock based on herd or group sentimentality.

➤ What should I pay attention to when doing research on stocks?

Read the earnings report and invest based on that. Check on the Company's Guidance where the Company executives talk about future growth and confidence levels based on existing income, productivity, and company debt levels.

Check for specific news where Institutional Investors like Morgan Stanley, the Banks, and large Private Financial Firms buying into specific stocks. They have the advantage of knowing better on specific company performance news than regular day traders. Such positive news should prompt you to purchase said stock, based on growth trend predicted for the foreseeable future, including global trade tensions if any, related to the stock.

➤ What is the **Bid Size**? (Additional info).

The Bid Size represents the QUANTITY of a stock that investors are willing to purchase at that specific Bid price. Remember, Bid Size and price can change any time.

➤ What is the **Ask Size**? (Additional info).

The Ask Size represents the QUANTITY of a stock that the Market Makers/Sellers are willing to offer for sale the shares at a specific Ask price. Remember, Ask Size and price can change any time.

➤ What is the **BID/ASK** size? (added info).

These numbers represent the aggregate number of pending trades at the present stock price. This helps you understand the demand for the stock at any given time. You could cross check this Bid/Ask Size with the present volume of shares being traded. It will help give you a different aspect of the trading scenario for that specified minute or hour.

Example: **PEP** - Pepsi, 400x300 as the Bid/Ask rate shows there is higher amount of Bids and lower Asks, at the given share price. The stock is down $-0.49 (-0.36%) Before 30 minutes it was 200x300 and now as I write it shows a possible reversal in the Bid/Ask Size and rise in demand (as of Jan 2, 2020).

Example: **CCL** - Carnival Corp, 500x400 as the Bid/Ask rate shows there is fewer buyers than sellers. Price of CCL $50.88 up $0.045 (0.09%) (as of Jan 2, 2020).

Example: **NIO** - Nio Electric Corp, Bid/Ask is 10600x12200 shows there are fewer buyers to bid for the stock, than those selling the stock, suggesting a drop in demand. Based on this drop in demand, you can see a corresponding drop in price for the stock. Price of NIO $3.65 is down $-0.37 (-9.20%) (as of Jan 2, 2020).

The rules of Economics state, the greater the demand, the shorter the supply, results in a higher price and vice versa.

Remember, these Bid/Ask Size numbers can change at any given time. This will however indicate the current trend, up or down price movement of the market. The Bid/Ask Size can be used as a reliable indicator among others.

➤ What if I am too scared or too excited to make a trade?

Don't trade on emotions. You can speak out aloud or write a paragraph or two in your journal the previous evening as you prepare for the next day's trade. Plan a course of action and mark your possible ENTRY and EXIT prices. Remember, the market may move too fast based on volatility, or really slow. Enter the stock market only if there is a good level of volatility. Don't trade if you're just plain bored.

➤ How many stocks should I trade any time?

MONEY TRADE STOCKS
JACOB DAVID

Trade between 1 to 3 stocks based on what you can handle, and how much cash you have to spare. Focusing on too many stocks may not be a great idea when you are starting off. Ideally, it is good to focus on 1 to 3 stocks. So if two stocks are sluggish come trade day, then you can focus all your energies on the 3rd stock. Research 3 to 5 stocks. Be prepared to trade 1 or 2 stocks based on various factors that this book discusses. Make notes later that evening why you made that particular trade.

➤ How much money should I invest in a stock if I am starting out?

Try not to invest more than 5% of your money into any given stock.

Example: If you have $1,000, invest $50/- (5%). Or if you are a risk-taker, and want to have an aggressive return, sure that you can pull it off, invest $250 or 25% into that stock. By investing 5%, what you are doing is learning how the stock market operates. If the stock goes in your favor, goes up, calculate your returns in percentage. Or, vice versa.

MONEY TRADE STOCKS
JACOB DAVID

Remember to write notes at the end of the day. Notes can be one line to two paragraphs.

➤ Should I write notes as soon as I buy or exit a position in the stock market?

No, focus on day trading or swing trading (holding for a few days to a few weeks). Write notes for each buy or sell transaction only the same evening. Remember to not spend more than 20 minutes for this activity each evening. You can access Order Status on your account to see the trades you bought or sold and the price per share, and time of day traded. I would also note the volume of shares traded (on average) for that day for each stock.

➤ Should I abandon writing notes once I feel confident enough or become an expert?

Writing notes help you organize your thoughts briefly on paper or on Word Doc. I would suggest writing notes for every trade, even if it is only 1 to 2 lines. You will find this to be helpful. But as you grow confident, writing notes helps you keep your confidence in check by not growing cocky or over confident.

Writing notes on each trade helps you to focus on each trade individually and helps collect your thoughts on each trade that you performed that particular day.

Also, remember to stay humble. There is no expert in this line of business. The knowledge you can learn in stock trading is infinite. So forget you are an expert at any time. You are always going to be a student, albeit, at a higher level, with lots more experience in the stock market, than when you first began.

➤ When should I exit a stock position?

If you are swing trading or day trading, exit as soon as you see a reversal in trend, a slow down in volatility levels, knowledge of some new piece of trading news, which can affect a stock's price. You buy and sell stocks if your goal is to make an income, without getting attached to any particular stock(s). Remember don't get married to a stock.

➤ How long should I hold a stock?

MONEY TRADE STOCKS
JACOB DAVID

If you are looking for a steady income through stock dividend and appreciation of stock price over a year or two years, buy good performing stocks that pay dividends after researching and hold them anywhere between 4 months to 2 years. The hold time period I leave to your discretion, based on the stock you purchase, the strength of the company's performance through earnings quarterly, and continued upward price trend.

➤ What about long-term investing?

If you have absolute good knowledge on a few stocks, like say, Amazon (AMZN), Google (GOOG), Chipotle Mexican Grill (CMG), Facebook (FB), McDonald's (MCD), Home Depot (HD), Deere (DE), Pepsi (PEP), Nvidia (NVDA), Coca-Cola (KO), then long-term investment with a goal to get a great return is advisable. People buy such stocks and hold for anywhere from 5 years to 20 years. Warren Buffett is one such individual who made great returns this way. However, as I always say, keep a watch over your money, your stock portfolio at least once or twice a week. Make sure you are in the know on news regards your stock portfolio, quarterly earnings, news regards company debt, performance news, and news regards key changes at the helm, executives leaving and joining the company.

Do long-term investing only if you have all the patience in the world. Buy and hold forever. Again, do your research. And stay on top of things. Keep a watch over your money.

➤ What are some of the **Quick Ways** to note and research healthy stocks? (Time Saver)

1. Check the Top-moving stocks list.
2. Check upcoming earnings for stocks.
3. Check the Top-Loser stocks list.
4. Check the Top stocks by sector.

Research stocks in each of these points 1 to 3. Point 3, When stocks lose value, they tend to go back up. Check for historical price patterns of highs and lows. Find out the reasons why the price dropped on a certain stock.

Keep a page for each stock to note down your personal thoughts, opinions, positives and negatives, including the date of note-making.

This can be done on a Word Doc, so you can revise the notes as needed, or refer to them at a later date.

Don't go about buying stocks based on social media hype. Do your own research. When reading articles make sure they are not paid or sponsored articles, but genuine stock analysis. Treat every article or blog with suspicion. Make your own confirmations and validate it with FACTS relating to that specific stock, based on direct company news.

If you need further confirmation, contact **Investor Relations** for the company, call or write them an email stating your concerns or questions you have that you want to clarify about their company BEFORE you invest.

➤ What if I make mistakes as I stock trade?

Everyone makes mistakes. We learn by making mistakes. I'd suggest you paper trade to get an idea of how the trader platform works. Make calls to your stock broker and clarify aspects of the platform that you are not sure about.

MONEY TRADE STOCKS
JACOB DAVID

As you become confident and start real trading, make sure to keep an online notebook to type in quick, short notes about your trade, your reflections, exit and entry points, and other relevant details, including what you learned as you traded, daily market reactions, what mistakes you made, and what things you did right. You can include or exclude anything.

The reason you keep this notebook is to organize the thoughts in your brain as you make these notes. Your brain has to work to think logically to write down what you just experienced while stock trading. As you do this daily, it helps your brain learn each trade and the many layers involved.

1. Keep the notes to two paragraphs.
2. Include the date of each trading day.
3. Include Stock Ticker and stock name.
4. Price entered trade + Commissions.
5. Number of Shares purchased.
6. Volume of shares traded at entry.
7. Price exited trade - Commissions.
8. Volume of shares traded at exit.
9. Subtract 6 from 4 for total made.

10. Number of hours/days/months held.
11. Percentage of Profit/Loss.
12. Amount of Profit/Loss made.
13. 10% Tithe - add the orange color to pay, change to Light Green when paid.
14. Notes Column
15. Explanation Column (optional).

Make an excel sheet with the relevant values above, starting from point 2, Date. In addition to writing notes, keeping an excel sheet will help you account for each trade, profit and loss made, which will help you with taxes.

You do not have to enter the trade in your excel sheet right away. You can check your order status page after you are finished trading for the day and enter the values in your excel sheet then. This way it does not disrupt your trading momentum.

However, make notes as soon as you can, while the trade is still fresh in your mind. You can break up the notes into two parts. Make notes when you buy the stock, write reasons as to your analysis on the stock, why you bought the stock and how many shares you purchased. Write down social sentiment, and market sentiment and any other relevant thought. In your second part, write down notes when you sell the stock, exit price, and market conditions then. Write down your reasons as to why you exited the market, and your analysis of the stock at the point of exit.

Regards, point 13, paying tithes is a Christian principle. So if you make $1.00 profit, you will have to give $0.10 for charitable causes.

If you are not a Christian, you can still donate 10% of your profit from stock trading to reputable charities that you believe in, so that it will help ease the suffering of men, women, and children, across the world, who don't have money or jobs, or the ability to live a blessed life like you and me. Or remember to invest money in a business to help underprivileged people get meaningful jobs.

Remember, when you give money, food, drink, clothes, shelter, and daily necessities, you feel good about yourself, you feel your life has a purpose and that your kind actions are benefiting others who are not so privileged like yourself.

MONEY TRADE STOCKS
JACOB DAVID

Questions about Jacob David, the author:

➤ Where am I from?

I am from Pondicherry, South India, born and raised. I was born in 1970.

➤ What is my background?

I have a Masters in American & English Literature from the University of Houston, Central Campus, graduate of 2002.

I also have a Masters of Philosophy in English Language Teaching (ELT) and a Masters in English & World Literature from the Pondicherry University, South India, a Graduate of 1993 and 1994. I am a two-time gold medalist in English Literature. I got my Bachelor's from Bishop Heber College, Trichy, South India.

I'd like to give credit where credit is due. My foundation in learning was laid strong early on when I attended 5th grade at St. George's

MONEY TRADE STOCKS
JACOB DAVID

Home in Ketti, South India, a British taught boarding school.

➤ What do I currently do?

I am a Real Estate Agent, licensed to transact business in Texas. I focus on the Southwest Houston market covering 8 cities. I help home owners list and sell homes, help buyers save money on homes, lots, and farm land, plus help execute 1 to 2 year leases for families.

To know more, visit "Homes in Houston Today" (.com)

I am also a Graphic Designer (self-taught) with 15 years of work experience in the Advertising and Publishing industry.

I have been helping local businesses in Houston, Texas, with their content creation, establishing brand identity, culture, and experience, social media interactive user engagement, designing promotional material, logos, and printing services, since 2007.

MONEY TRADE STOCKS
JACOB DAVID

To know more, visit "Cafy Designs" Visit www.cafydesigns.com.

I put my Literature degree to good use, by writing content for social media, business websites, articles, and books.

➤ How long have I been trading?

I have been trading for over 10 plus years.

➤ What are some of the worst stock trades I have made?

Two in particular. Trading shares of SUBB (OTC - Suburban Minerals Corp) and shares of ACLH (OTC - Act Clean Technologies,) both lost value and became zero. Both these stocks were bought within the first few years of my trading. I must admit that I did not take trading seriously. I completely forgot about these stocks for a few years.

When I returned, I was shocked to find that both these stocks lost value and had become zero. That's what woke me up. I started paying attention to stocks more often and learning how to trade better.

➤ What are some of the best stock trades I have made?

PEP - Pepsi, (NASDAQ) each share that I purchased at $97.17 and the stock went up 33.7% to $130.00, a difference of $33.83 per share in 12 months. This stock pays dividends of 2.95% or $3.82 per share, annually.

BE - Bloom Energy, (NYSE) offered its IPO, each share at $15 which then shot up 153% to $38, a difference of $23 per share in about six months. This stock does not pay dividends.

The above two are examples of best trades.

➤ What is your earliest introduction to stocks?

When I was 8 years old, a family friend, Paul uncle used to talk to my dad about stocks. I used to listen intently. Later, I used to ask questions about the stock market to my dad. He was patient with me and explained what shares were, what a stock was, and how it is traded on the stock exchange. This increased my interest in learning about stocks. I always kept thinking about the stock market and kept looking into good blue chip Indian stock companies like Ashok Leyland, Asian Paints, Bajaj Motors, Eicher Motors, Godrej Appliances, Hindustan Motors, Hindustan Unilever, Tata Motors, and Tata Steel to name a few.

➤ Would I consider myself an expert in stock trading?

No. I am a student of stock trading. I have been learning for the last 15 years, since 2004. From reading books to watching specific stock subject videos on YouTube, every weekday, every weekend, whenever I find time, I educated myself on stocks and the stock market. Making notes as I learn each day has helped me understand the stock market better.

➤ Why did you write this book "MONEY TRADE STOCKS" ?

Growing up, I was taught how to handle money early on. My dad helped me open a bank account when I was 17. My mom taught me how to handle currency. They both quizzed me on shopping and how much change would the shopkeeper give me in different scenarios.

I realize that Financial education is direly needed in today's society, in a big way. Students in high schools are never taught about the stock market or how the stock market works. They are never taught how to open a Money Market Savings account at a local bank.

I realized that by writing a book on the stock market from a beginner's point of view, this would fill that void. No question is less important. No question is stupid. Every question helps us understand how the stock market works. It's interesting to learn about the stock market, in stages and in layers.

In March 2019, I was reading the reviews of stock trading books available on the market. Many reviews left by readers were negative saying that those books were a rip-off and did not teach much about stocks or trading itself.

These comments got me thinking. "I have been learning about the stock market for the last 15 years. Why don't I put what I have learned in the form of a book?" I asked myself.

So this led me to write this book. I wrote it from the viewpoint of any trader, putting myself in their shoes, asking and answering those questions, I had as a beginner and what I learned advancing forward. I remember the challenges I faced learning the ins and outs of the stock market. Writing this book gave me a better understanding of what each student would face trying to trade the stock market.

I have also gone beyond by doing further research to provide answers to questions that can help broaden everyone's understanding of the stock market in a simple and easy way.

The questions and answers in this book will help educate traders of the stock market at different levels.

This book helps you go swimming in the ocean of trading. Remember to keep educating yourself daily. Read those books you can find on the stock market, based on good reviews.

MONEY TRADE STOCKS
JACOB DAVID

➤ Why is this book in a Question & Answer format?

The Question and Answer format is easy to handle for most readers who are learning about the stock market. They want answers in capsule form, and not big chapters of hard to find information. Your Time is precious, and I understand that you'd like to learn fast and start trading as soon as possible.

Learning about stocks can get to be a heavy and dry subject. People tend to lose interest and get distracted easily.

People want to get to the point right away. Besides, people who know the answers to some questions, can feel free to skip those questions and move ahead. This book is written to provide complete freedom to you, the reader. You get to choose what you want to read and when. You get to set the pace.

Finally, I tried reading books written in the chapter format. I found that I kept losing interest, got easily distracted, when the author rambled on, and fell asleep many times.

I so wished there was a book in Q&A format. Simple, quick, easy to learn. I realized that there must be other people just like me, who'd like to learn in short capsules. So I chose the Question & Answer format.

➤ How can you show your appreciation as a reader for the information presented in this book?

First, please remember to leave a 5 star review if this book has helped you in someway.

Remember, your review is very important, as it informs other buyers about the quality of information in my book. It helps them buy this book, learn from it, and secure their financial futures. Your honest review will actually help them make an informed purchase. Thank you.

Second, please send me feedback. I'd love to read your feedback. Please use a Subject Line: Money Trade Stocks Book Feedback.

MONEY TRADE STOCKS
JACOB DAVID

My Email: creative ads for you @ yahoo.com

Third, share information about this book "**Money Trade Stocks**" on social media. It will help others learn about the stock market by reading this book. Share the Amazon link.

Thank you for purchasing this book. I wish you a Happy New Decade!

This copy is the Second Edition: January 2020.

_____

MONEY TRADE STOCKS
JACOB DAVID

My Notes
(What do I need to further research on?)

www.ingramcontent.com/pod-product-compliance
Lightning Source LLC
Chambersburg PA
CBHW021823170526
45157CB00007B/2672